My Life as a
Middle School
Mom

My Life as a Middle School Mom

My kids may be deductible, but they're still taxing!

Angela Elwell Hunt

VINE
BOOKS

SERVANT PUBLICATIONS
ANN ARBOR, MICHIGAN

Unless otherwise indicated, Scripture quotations are taken from the *Holy
Bible*, New Living Translation, © 1996. Used by permission of Tyndale
House Publishers, Inc., Wheaton, Illinois 60189. All rights reserved.

In some cases, names and identifying characteristics have been changed to
protect the privacy of the individuals whose stories are told in this book.
Actual names and stories have been used with express written permission.

Published by Servant Publications
P.O. Box 8617
Ann Arbor, Michigan 48107

Cover design: Paz Design Group
Cover illustration: Chris Sharp

00 01 02 03   10 9 8 7 6 5 4 3 2 1

Printed in the United States of America
ISBN 1-56955-108-1

LIBRARY OF CONGRESS CATALOGING-IN-PUBLICATION DATA

Hunt, Angela Elwell, 1957-
    My life as a middle school mom : my kids may be deductible, but
    they're still taxing! / by Angela Elwell Hunt.
        p   cm.
    ISBN 1-56955-108-1 (alk. paper)
    1. Mothers—Religious life.   2. Middle school students—Religious life.
    3. Parenting—Religious aspects—Christianity.   I. Title.
    BV4529.18.H86 2000
    248.8'431—dc21   00-029009

This book is dedicated to Gary Hunt,
who has led me into more adventure than
any woman has a right to expect ...
in one lifetime, at least.

I love you, honey.

Introduction

I do the taxes in our family. The business stuff I hand over to an accountant, but I find a perverse pleasure in printing our financial records at the end of the year and discovering that we contributed $673.17 to support various Pizza Hut delivery persons. My kids may not be getting home-cooked meals every night, but we keep the pizza people in business!

At tax time I especially love itemizing deductions. Medical and dental expenses, taxes paid, interest paid, and gifts to the church and other charitable organizations ... those deductions add up quickly. After subtracting all those assorted deductions from gross income, I'm then allowed to deduct a healthy chunk for my two darling children. What follows is an annual ritual—with my tax papers in hand, I look at the figures on my 1040 and wish I had more kids.

For a single golden moment, I smile as visions of tax deductions and baby booties dance in my head, then I recall the gray roots sprouting out of my skull. Reality asserts itself, and I remember that my quiver is full. Quite.

Don't get me wrong—I love my kids. I prayed hard to get them, and I'm praying hard to *keep* them. As I write this, they are fifteen and sixteen, a boy and a girl. I'd tell you their names, but then they'd accuse me of embarrassing them in public. So for this book they shall remain nameless and as protected as possible. Living with a writer-mother and a youth pastor-father is trial enough, so I try to cut them some slack when I can.

In addition to the two young adults I parent, I'm a part-time mother figure for scores of middle school students at our large church. I married into the youth ministry, you see, and I've been a youth pastor's wife since 1980. Over the past twenty years I've hugged sobbing girls, rebuked mischievous boys, and occasionally taken kids in for the night when they and their biological parents weren't speaking. I've seen middle schoolers at their worst ... and at their best. It's a very special age.

I never intended to be a surrogate mother for more than fifteen hundred middle schoolers. For a while I wondered if I would be a mother at all, or even a wife. At twenty-one, I was a student at Liberty University, working hard to get my English degree, and traveling the world with one of the college's musical ensembles. I wanted to get married, of course (I had bought a complete set of Revere Ware for my hope chest at age fifteen), but by the time I reached twenty I realized that waiting on God meant not rushing into one relationship after another. If he wanted to wait a while before bringing Mr. Right into my life, that was okay.

One afternoon I looked across the church gym and saw Gary Hunt surrounded by a clutch of middle school girls. The aforementioned Mr. Hunt intrigued me for several reasons—first, he was Old—nearly thirty, if rumors could be trusted. Second, middle school students are notoriously blunt, and they can see through any façade. So Mr. Hunt had to be transparent and honestly likeable, or those girls wouldn't have given him the time of day. Third, he was tall. At five foot nine inches myself, tall was a plus. Fourth, I'd heard he was a good basketball player. (Actually, his basketball ability made not one whit of difference to me, but he would want me to mention it.)

To make a long story short, a couple of our friends did some conniving and Gary and I began to date. Within nine months we were engaged, and within eighteen months we were married. I knew Gary felt called by God to minister to early adolescents— the junior high years were a turning point for him, the age when he had left the things he'd been taught and wandered away from God. He wanted to spend his life working with middle school students so other kids wouldn't go through the same thing.

Fine, I thought. Middle schoolers were just older elementary students, right? I'd practically grown up in church, moving through Vacation Bible School and Sunday school as a child, then spending my teenage years working with the younger kids. I knew all the words to "Climb, Climb up Sunshine Mountain" and I never, *ever* sang the words when you're supposed to substitute *hmmm* and *hmmm* in "Deep and Wide." If anybody had ever been prepped and primed for middle school ministry, I thought, I had.

So I graduated from college on May 12 and married a middle school pastor on May 13. We spent our honeymoon in Gatlinburg, Tennessee, then I came home, ready and willing to play the role of pastor's wife and middle school mom.

I soon discovered that I'd made a couple of false assumptions. First, no one wanted to consider me a mature pastor's wife at age twenty-two, no matter how Old my husband was. Second, the middle schoolers didn't see me as Gary's wife. The middle school girls saw me as the Other Woman.

Middle school, you see, is an age of extreme hero worship and severe adolescent crushes. There were at least three middle school girls who considered my husband their best friend. They telephoned him every night without fail, spoke for nearly an hour, and wrote him ardent notes assuring him of their love and affection—sprinkled, of course, with just enough "I love Jesus" comments to keep things on a spiritual level. They sat with us in church, the three of them jostling for position on Gary's right side while I stewed on his left. Starlight twinkled in their gazes when they looked at him; flat, cold resentment filled their eyes when—*if*—they looked at me.

Yes, my husband was Old in those days—nearly thirty—but I never said he was perfect and complete. He had only been a Christian five years, and in some ways the ministry was newer to him than to me. So when I tried to talk to him about my feelings, he would respond with, "But, honey, you knew you were marrying a youth pastor!" My irritation grew into resentment, then into bitterness. Quite frankly, my stomach began to knot at the mere *sight* of a middle school student.

I was anything *but* a loving middle school pastor's wife.

I don't know how long we'd been married—probably about nine months—when I went on a trip with a friend and poured out my heart. I thank God that she shared my feelings with one of Gary's best friends, who then sat my young husband down and said, "You're going to lose your wife."

My husband may have been young in the ministry, but he was wise. Coming from someone else, the words sank into his heart, and for the first time he understood. He came home, apologized, and together we resolved to make some changes.

The marathon telephone sessions stopped; he was always available to kids at the office and for emergencies, but not at home. He began to spread his attention among a large number of kids instead of just a few, so his ministry expanded. And he realized that middle school infatuation, though it's usually harmless, does very little to help young people develop spiritually.

I, in turn, relaxed and realized that happiness did not depend upon having my husband all to myself for several hours a day. I also began to enjoy middle school ministry again. I developed special programs for the girls, I helped "coach" Gary's Little League team when he had to be away, and I began to see middle grade students for what they are—not big kids or teens in training, but charming, honest people in a unique span of life. They are "tweens," in between childhood and maturity, and there's no creature on God's earth quite like a tweenager.

Today I enjoy meeting tweens, whether at church or at book signings. I can identify a sixth-, seventh-, or eighth-grader from across the room—they have a unique look I've come to recognize. After parenting a tween, you'll begin to recognize the look, too.

I shared the preceding information so that you'll understand that my life as a middle school mom didn't come easily or naturally. Eight years into our marriage and ministry, when our children were two and three years old, Gary and I wrote a book about how to parent tweenagers. I remember an afternoon when our pastor looked at us with a twinkle in his eye and asked how we could write a book about parenting middle schoolers when we didn't have any children that age. "Oh," I replied breezily, "we've had *hundreds*. In our years of middle school ministry, we've encountered just about every situation you can imagine."

Now that my children are fifteen and sixteen, I understand the reason for the twinkle in my pastor's eye—and I've come to believe that advice from *anyone* who has not walked in the path of experience is highly suspect. It's one thing to talk objectively about a topic; it's quite another to experience it.

Objectivity is useful, but practical experience is far more valuable.

I'm well aware that there are no easy solutions to parenting problems. The longer I'm a parent, the more often I realize that I don't have the answers. I can't solve your parenting problems, and you can't solve mine. What we *can* do is share stories of "battlefield experience," learn some guiding scriptural principles, and pray for guidance. In a way, we're all parenting by Braille, feeling our way in the dark and searching for the Right Thing to Do.

The pages to come are stuffed with stories and sprinkled with observations—with a dash of instruction and flavorful footnotes thrown in to prove I'm not pulling facts and ideas out of thin air. Though most of the following stories are written in the first person, they did not all spring from my family. A few are composites of situations I've encountered over the years. Some of the stories are mine, some came from other moms and dads, and only the Lord and I know which are which. *All* of the names have been changed to protect the immature.

I owe a special word of thanks to my friends Terri Blackstock, Connie Mayes, Deb Raney, Sherry Wilt, Carolyn Pizutti, Keith Scott, and Francine Rivers for sharing stories and thoughts from their own lives.

So prop up your feet on the ottoman or coffee table (go ahead, no one's looking!), grab a diet soda or cup of coffee, and settle back to enjoy these A to Z stories of middle school motherhood.

Academics

In a somewhat ironic twist, your tween's brain will begin to develop in new ways just as his interest in academics begins to wane. Researchers have shown that schoolwork becomes decreasingly significant as tweens progress from elementary and middle school to the ninth grade. Meeting parents' standards for good grades is relatively unimportant to early adolescents, though they do focus on their schoolwork in the later high school years—just in time to prepare for SATs and college entrance exams.[1]

In one study of tweens, researchers found that ninth-grade girls spent far more time talking about their friends than about school. Of all activities done at home, ninth-grade girls spent more time on *personal grooming* than on anything else, including homework.

So if your straight-A student brings home a few B's in the eighth grade, don't get upset. Her focus is merely shifting for a while.

Acne

Your emerging adolescent may find that his face breaks out often or only occasionally. If your child has a persistent case of acne, don't assume that avoiding chocolate or fried foods will solve the problem. The cause is rooted in hormones, not food, and a dermatologist can work wonders for your child.

Don't let your child suffer through taunts of "Zit-face" or "pimple picker." Take him to the doctor.

Adolescence

Once I picked up the phone and heard my friend Phyllis' worried voice. "I need help," she said, her tone flat. "I don't know what to do. My daughter went into her bedroom last Friday night and came out a different person. She's moody, she's grumpy, and she's selfish. What happened?"

Nothing that hasn't happened to all of us. The tweenage years—sixth, seventh, and eighth grades—have arrived and brought with them a confusing array of conflicting emotions, habits, and friendships.

Tweens are too old to ride their bikes, and too young to drive. They're too mature for Ronald McDonald, and too immature for dating. They're caught between the innocence of childhood and the sophistication of high school.

Strictly speaking, adolescence begins at puberty, and puberty arrives earlier today than it did when we were kids. According to a study published in the October 1999 issue of *Pediatrics*, most girls today show signs of puberty before the age of ten. At the turn of the twentieth century, puberty didn't begin to arrive until age fifteen.[2]

Each child encounters adolescence on his or her individual timetable. More pervasive than a biological clock, however, are the influences of older teens and television. The rites of passage between childhood and maturity will still influence kids who are years away from puberty. Marcel Danesi, author of *Cool, The Signs and Meanings of Adolescence*, says that children are "becoming teenagers much younger and they're staying there much longer. The cultural aspects of teens are picked up much earlier now than the physical ones."[3]

What cultural aspects are tweens adopting? According to Elaine Carey of *The Toronto Star*, "they all want cell phones but pagers will do in a pinch, although they don't seem to know why they want them. It just looks cool.... The girls wear make-up ... and they never have enough money." One tween told Carey, "I'm going to marry a really rich guy, then divorce him and marry for love. But first I'm going to have his kids so I get child support."[4]

I can only pray she was kidding.

The Alarm Clock Curfew Solution

When your tween or teenager has a late curfew and you're so tired you just *know* you're going to fall asleep, settle the problem of monitoring with an alarm clock. Set the clock for the time your tween or teen is supposed to be home, and tell him to turn off the alarm when he comes in. Then allow yourself the luxury of sleep. If the alarm goes off, however, and the wandering child is not home, you'll be up, awake, and watching the door!

One caveat: one mother told me that she knew of a situation where the teens went home, turned off the alarm, and went back out again. If your child has proven less than trustworthy, better have a backup alarm under your pillow!

Allowance

I'm a big believer in not giving or accepting something for nothing. During our first year of marriage, we accepted an offer from a vacuum company—just for listening to a demonstration, we were supposed to get our living room carpet cleaned. So we invited the salesman over, slid our mismatched furniture out of the living room, and sat back to enjoy a freshly cleaned, sweet-smelling carpet.

You can probably guess what happened. The man came over, showed us his handy-dandy machine, and then offered to give us more for our old vacuum than I had paid for it six months before! The shiny new machine did everything but balance a checkbook, but the price was way out of our budget. Not to be dissuaded, the salesman called his boss, who (so graciously!) allowed him to offer us an even better deal.

We still couldn't afford it. Not to worry: the salesman got back on the phone and arranged for the sweetest financing package ever offered on the face of the planet. Overwhelmed with feelings of unworthiness, we signed on the dotted line, then noticed that it was nearly 10 P.M. Noticing the late hour, the salesman left, promising to come back another day to shampoo the living room rug.

Our carpet stayed dirty, and about forty-eight hours later we realized we had swallowed bait, hook, and the longest line imaginable. After that, Gary and I decided that we'd never again accept a free in-home demonstration. There is almost always a string attached.

I carried this lesson into parenting. I didn't want my children to think money grew on the parent tree, so my kids had to perform a few chores in order to receive their allowance. But, like all moms, most of the time I ended up doing their chores myself because it's easier, faster, and more efficient to *just do it* than to nag.

Something was definitely wrong with this arrangement. So Gary and I sat down and talked about what we wanted to achieve with the allowance system. We came up with three goals. We wanted our children to:

- Complete their household chores,
- Do their homework, and
- Not beat each other up.

Once we had formulated our goals, I went on a shopping expedition and searched for poker chips—not the sort of thing that a pastor's wife buys every day. Once I found them, Gary and I called the kids together.

"The allowance system is changing," Gary announced. "We will always cover your meals, clothes, and activities—we do those things because you are part of this family. But if you want extra spending money, here's how to earn it: From this day forward you will earn chips every night. If you make your bed every morning and do your chores, you will earn one white chip worth twenty-five cents. If you do your homework after school, you will earn a blue chip worth fifty cents. If you can make it through the day without insulting or hitting each other, you will earn a red chip worth one dollar."

My children sat in silence, but I could see their mental calculators adding up the numbers. "If you earn all three chips every day for a week," I added, "you can cash them in and earn $12.25. Not a bad weekly allowance, but you'll have to keep your part of the bargain to earn the full amount."

The result? The system worked like a charm until we parents got lazy and forgot to award the chips at the end of each day. When the ceremony ended, so did the chips' significance, and soon I was finding poker chips under beds and in candy dishes. When we stopped placing priority on the system, so did the kids.

The moral of this story: you get what you honor. Establish a system and stick to it, and you just might see results.

Attractiveness and Popularity

"If you're not beguiling by age twelve, forget it."

Lucy (Charles Schulz)[5]

If you're wondering why your tweenage son and daughter spend what seems like an inordinate amount of time in front of the bathroom mirror, here's a clue: Personal attractiveness is *the* most important factor in determining a student's popularity and success with his peers.

Yes, physical beauty is superficial. Yes, it's sad that our culture places such an emphasis on outward appearance. But neither of those truths changes the fact that attractiveness counts in the tween world. (Are things terribly different in the realm of adults?)

In a psychological study of 270 ninth-graders between fourteen and fifteen years old, students were offered a choice of hypothetical study partners who were (1) attractive with good grades, (2) attractive with low grades, (3) unattractive with good grades, or (4) unattractive with low grades.

The result? Attractiveness was *the* most important factor in the lab partner's desirability. When the partner's attractiveness was high, his desirability was high. When the partner's attractiveness was low, his desirability was low, regardless of academic performance.[6]

Studies have also shown that tween girls tend to emphasize their peers' attractiveness, social skills, and academic success, while boys judge their peers' popularity by achievement in sports, "coolness" or "toughness," and success with the opposite sex.[7] In all studies, attractiveness and popularity go hand in hand.

I'm not including this information in order to foster superficiality, but I do think it's important that we understand the world revolving around our kids. If we can do anything to help our children cope—finance the orthodontia, buy the stylish outfit, allow the popular haircut—we'll be doing a lot to help our tweens survive in a middle school environment. Don't compromise important standards, but if a little sprucing up won't hurt, help your child feel as attractive as he can.

Bad Language

I received the shock of my life the other day when I was working on the family computer. We have a program installed that captures every keystroke (it's designed to back up your work in case of power failure), and when the power went on and off, I had to use the backup program to recapture the paragraphs I'd just typed.

Along with my work, the computer also displayed some e-mail messages my twelve-year-old daughter had sent to her friends. I gaped in amazement as I read words my daughter would never dare use at home. They weren't exactly curse words, but vulgar words that shouldn't be a part of any Christian's vocabulary.

I sat back and closed my eyes, wondering how I should handle the situation, and then I realized something: the words that had upset me were words that have appeared on prime-time television in the past five years. Yes, they're vulgar, and my daughter never hears her father or me use that kind of language. But when she's being cool with her friends, I can see why she'd want to mimic the vocabulary she hears on television....

I will talk to my daughter. If she knew where these words came from and what they really mean, I know she'd think twice about using them....

A frantic mother once caught me in the hall at church. "I'm a basket case," she said, thrusting a note into my hand. "My ten-year-old, a Christian who knows better, wrote this!"

I glanced at the note, and saw that the boy had written an unprintable profanity in large letters. I gave the note back to her and suggested that she calm down, then find a time to study the third chapter of James with her son. The key verse is James 3:10: "And so blessing and cursing come pouring out of the same mouth. Surely, my brothers and sisters, this is not right!"

Our children need to learn how to control the words they write and speak, but parents should not be surprised when inappropriate words begin to pop up in a child's language. Tweens use vulgar words because they hear adults using the same words on television, in the movies, and even at home. They use bad language because they want to feel and act grown up.

Kids with the best intentions try to find ways to interject a little "adult" language into their conversations. James, a strong Christian tween raised in a Christian family, once used a vulgar word as he was talking to Gary. "Why, James!" Gary said. "What kind of language is that?"

James blushed. "I heard my brother say it once. Then I tried it out on my dad and he didn't say anything."

"Your dad must not have been listening," Gary answered. "I'm sure that is not a word he would like you to use. More important, that word refers to an activity that dishonors Christ. I know the Lord would not want you to use that word."

Tweens use "shock words" among themselves because these words are part of their own special language—a language they don't use at home or at church. And profanity is one of the hardest habits for a tweenage boy to control.

After our country-western jamboree and its attendant mud fight, Gary was hosing mud from a group of boys' feet. Another boy was standing too close, and Gary accidentally splashed water on his Reeboks. "Jee-sus Christ!" yelled the boy.

When Gary corrected him, the boy looked up in blank innocence. "You mean that's wrong?"

You might think a churchgoing kid would know not to take the Lord's name in vain, but tweens hear our Lord's name used in anger a lot more often than they hear lessons on the third commandment.

My husband, bless his heart, was a typical wild and woolly boy who didn't turn to the Lord until he was twenty-five. He tells me that once he was playing basketball while his parents watched from the stands. His father was really into the game, cheering and yelling with all the others, but his mother, who was deaf and read lips, was more reserved. She sat quietly and watched the game. At one point, however, when someone slapped the ball away and Gary uttered a bad word, his mother leaned forward intently. When they got home, she lit into him. "Gary Allan Hunt," she said, her eyes blazing with rebuke. "I saw what you said!"

Don't be afraid to correct your tween's language ... even if it means explaining exactly why a word is inappropriate in polite conversation. But be careful—your children are listening to *your* speech, too.

Belching

We didn't plan to get arrested—we were just going out for a nice lunch at a local seafood restaurant. The hostess, seeing that we were four adults and a tween, sat us in a far corner of the restaurant and against the wall.

My son, Tommy, was a little more excited than usual because we had Scott and Joe with us, two young men who would be working with my husband for the coming months. Tommy is always active and loud when he's feeling comfortable, and he was feeling plenty comfortable with Mom and Dad and the older guys.

As we studied the menu, I looked around the small room where we'd been seated. There were three other tables in the area, and at the table next to us a uniformed deputy sheriff was eat-

ing lunch with two women. He was young, as were the women, and I couldn't tell if he was married to either of them. Beyond the deputy's table were two other tables, both occupied by older folks.

Tommy jabbered about this and that, trying to monopolize Scott and Joe's attention while we studied the menu. I called him down a couple of times, but I knew exactly what he was doing—showing off. Middle school students look up to older kids, and Tommy wanted to impress the older guys. His enthusiasm was practically squirting out of his ears.

The waitress came, took our orders and then our menus. The three men became involved in a conversation about something or other (probably sports), while I stared out the window.

And then Tommy burped.

There was a moment of horrified silence, then one of the older folks yelled, "Good one, kid!" I covered my face with my hand, Father glared at son, and Joe and Scott tried not to laugh. Tommy apologized, though his expression clearly revealed his pride in such a window-rattling belch.

I shook my head, too weary to count the times I'd reprimanded the boy for burping in public. He knew it was bad manners, he knew it was against The Rules, but it got results! Joe and Scott were staring at him with wide eyes.

I couldn't believe it when the deputy sheriff stood and came to our table, his hands resting on his belt. I don't remember his exact words, but he was clearly displeased.

"I'm sorry, sir," I said, thinking that he was coming over merely to intimidate Tommy into better manners. "I don't think it will happen again."

He must have seen something in my eyes, because he narrowed his gaze. "I'm not kidding," he said. "I could take you in for this kind of thing."

My embarrassment veered quickly to downright astonishment. Take us to jail? For public burping?

We stuttered our apologies, said it wouldn't happen again, then sat in stunned silence as the deputy strutted back to his table and took his seat with the women. Round-eyed with wonder, I turned to my husband. "I don't believe what just happened."

"Don't worry about it, honey," he answered. "He's just showing off for the women."

For the record, Tommy was suitably embarrassed, too, and that seemed to end the public burping ... at least I hope it did!

Believers on Campus

A tween's world revolves around home and school, so if your Christian child doesn't know any Christians at his school, he may feel like a missionary to the most forbidding place on earth. Ask your youth pastor to introduce your tween to other Christian kids who will be attending the same school. Inquire about before-school prayer groups or meetings of the Fellowship of Christian Athletes (FCA). Even though they may not have classes together, Christian kids can see each other in the halls and take comfort in knowing that they are not alone.

Several tweens in our church have begun before-school prayer meetings on their middle school campuses. They meet once a week to support and pray for one another, and the resulting sense of solidarity helps them feel a little less lost when school becomes overwhelming. See You At the Pole, an annual event usually held before school on a September Wednesday, is another great opportunity for your Christian tween to meet other believers on his campus.

Boring

What *isn't* boring in the tween years? I'm sure you've seen the living personification of boredom—the boy who paces through the house with a long face or the girl who can't seem to find a constructive way to spend her time. When you suggest going outside, reading a book, or cleaning the bedroom, you're likely to get the same answer: "That's boring."

The b-word can also come into play when you bring up a difficult subject at the dinner table. After the massacre at Columbine High School, hundreds of parents were shocked when their teens didn't want to talk about the massacre because the subject was *boring*.

Boring?

Don't panic, friends. Your child has not become so hard-hearted that a terrible tragedy leaves him feeling nothing. It's far more likely that you are misinterpreting your child's response.

According to Jean Perron, a teacher at Sun Prairie Middle School in Wisconsin, *boring* is one of those words that can have many meanings. Boring can mean:

- This actually is quite dull,
- I don't get this and I don't want to ask for help because then I'll *really* look stupid,
- This is too challenging and I don't want to risk my shaky self-esteem and possibly fall flat on my face, or:
- This topic scares the willies out of me, and I'd prefer not to deal with it right now.[8]

When a child's *boring* seems to imply the latter situation, we need to be careful and consider our conversation. When our children begin to use grown-up words and voice grown-up thoughts, we often think they can handle grown-up concepts. Sometimes they can't. They are standing on the edge of the world's stage, wanting desperately to believe they can make it by themselves, but stories of tragedy have populated the darkness beyond with nightmares and bogeymen. Our children want to believe the world is a wide and wonderful place, but we send them out the door after warning them about sexual predators, kidnappers, and serial killers.

How can we protect our children and yet be realistic? The answer lies in balance. The media tends to focus on bad news, so make sure your tween knows about the coach who won an award for his work with youth, the hero who risked his life to save a child from a burning building, the cleaning woman who saved her money in order to send poor students to college. Make certain your kid knows there are good people in the world who can be trusted to help.

Boundaries

We have three dogs, but one of them, Sadie, is an official man-eater. She's 150 pounds of pure aggression when she's afraid or feeling threatened. She loves our family, she loves a couple of friends who visit regularly, but if anyone else comes into our home, she's stiff-necked and snarling with fear.

The first and only time Sadie actually bit someone, I knew we had to take action. So I called a canine psychotherapist (I'm not joking), and for the next twelve weeks the doggie shrink and I worked with her. As part of Sadie's therapy, I had to get friends outside the family to come over and feed her twice a day (they fed her from the other side of a tall fence). During those twelve weeks, I wasn't allowed to pet, feed, or comfort her in any way. Sadie was supposed to learn that Strangers Are Good, but she proved to be a slow and undependable student. Now we put her away in a safe place whenever people come to visit.

Before we put in the tall fence, however, I investigated those "invisible fences" designed for dogs. For the invisible fence to work, you have to bury an electric line around the perimeter of your property, and your dog must wear a special collar. When the system is functioning properly, your dog will receive a slight shock when he nears the electric line, so he learns to respect the invisible boundary.

Before Sadie's problems fully blossomed, I thought the invisible fence sounded like a fine idea. I ordered a fencing system, then, after the box arrived, I read the fine print. The first notice on the back of the box was a warning that the system tended to short out in areas with frequent lightning strikes (we live in the lightning capital of the United States). The second notice said, *"The system will not deter any dog determined to escape the property."*

My dogs are *always* determined to escape the property. And with Sadie's aggression problem, I knew I couldn't risk injury to some innocent passerby. I boxed up the invisible fence and sent it back.

And now, as I'm thinking about fences and boundaries, I realize that children and dogs have at least one thing in common: for their own protection and for the safety of others, they need boundaries.

Setting boundaries, or reasonable rules, demonstrates your love to your children. Your child wants a curfew; he wants to know that you will not allow him to go certain places or see certain movies. Your daughter is quietly *relieved* when she can say, "I can't go to that concert. My mother would throw a fit if she found out."

But boundaries, like electronic fences, will not deter any child determined to escape parental authority. Children who are learning the difference between right and wrong can always choose wrong. When they do, "a foolish child brings grief to a father and bitterness to a mother" (Proverbs 17:25).

When your children make wrong decisions, remember the counsel of Proverbs 22:15: "A youngster's heart is filled with foolishness, but discipline will drive it away." Take whatever disciplinary steps are appropriate and necessary so your child will learn that it's far better to remain safe and protected inside the fence.

And remember—Solomon's proverbs, like the advice in this book, are *probabilities*, not gold-plated, instant-acting *promises*. Men and women, tweens and teens, have free will. They can always choose wrong as well as right.

Bras

> My eleven-year-old daughter mopes around the house all day waiting for her breasts to grow.
>
> Bill Cosby[9]

My little Marianne, now eleven, has been giving me a lot of chuckles lately. She started wanting to wear a bra because all of her friends were wearing them. I didn't think this fascination would last a week, but it has. The other day, she told me she needed a strapless bra for the occasions when she wanted to wear a shirt with spaghetti straps. I gently told her that she could probably get away with going braless when she wore those (since she's as flat as a board!). The idea hadn't occurred to her.

Lately she's gotten interested in shaving her legs, rolling her hair, and carefully coordinating her outfits. Last year she didn't care about any of those things. My older daughter keeps snickering and saying, "Mom, she's turning into a girl."

Funny how all this seems to happen overnight.

Cell Phones

As a parent, I've got to believe that cellular phones are the best invention of the last ten years. If you have one, when your tween wants to go to the mall with her friends, send the phone along and tell her to *turn it on*. That way you and your child will be in touch, and you'll rest easier.

When Church is Boring

"My kid doesn't want to go to church with us anymore," more than one parent has told me. "He says the services are boring. Sometimes I think I should require him to go to church, but I don't want to turn him off to spiritual things by demanding church attendance. What do I do?"

If you're in a church where the youth department is exciting and active, it's likely that your tween wants to go to church more often than you want to take him! But some kids balk at attending church with their families.

I would suggest two things: first, find a church that your child does enjoy. There is no reason your child *should* enjoy church if it's geared toward adults of another generation. Remember, you will have your children at home for *only a few more years*—so if moving to another church will keep your children interested in spiritual things, by all means, move your membership. Your kids will be out of the house soon enough; you can always move back to the church that suits you best.

Second, if you attend an active, youth-oriented church and are still faced with a reluctant churchgoer, require your tween to attend just one service per week with your family. Tell him or her that in order for *you* to be faithful to the Lord's command, you feel it is your responsibility to lead the family in church attendance.

If there is no youth-oriented church in your area, there are bound to be other options. Perhaps another church has a good youth program on Wednesday nights. You may find active programs sponsored by Campus Life, the Fellowship of Christian Athletes, Youth for Christ, Young Life, or Campus Crusade for Christ—look around your community and see what options are available. Thousands of Christian youth workers have invested their lives in making sure the gospel is relevant and exciting for tweens and teens, including *yours*.

Classy Womanhood

The sitcom ended to canned applause, and I rolled off the couch, ready to do my usual garbage collection sweep through the living room as I headed toward the kitchen. Suddenly the sitcom mother's image filled the screen—she was slender and designer-dressed, and every hair lay obediently in place. I could almost smell her expensive designer perfume.

I sniffed my hands. Eau de Wet Dog, mingled with the scents of supper.

"She's too classy to be real," I said, glaring at the woman on the television screen.

My husband lifted his brows.

"I mean, have you ever thought about it?" I continued. "There's not a mother alive who is that classy."

After all:

- *Classy women never show their toes in public. Mothers go barefoot as often as they can. In the winter they wear socks, even when they step out to fetch the newspaper from the driveway.*
- *Classy women are always dressed up. Mothers don't comb their hair before lunch on Saturday, and they undo that waistband button the moment they come through the front door.*

- Classy women *never yell. Mothers screech like loons when their children are bleeding, playing football, or about to do something they aren't supposed to do.*
- Classy women *read newspapers and ten-pound tomes on the* New York Times *best-seller list. Mothers read comics first thing in the morning and Dear Abby at lunch. At bedtime, mothers read dog-eared books about how to discipline their children properly.*
- Classy women *do not eat leftovers from their children's plates or lick the spoon after mixing chocolate icing. Mothers do, and consequently gain two pounds per child per year for the rest of their lives.*
- Classy women *cook exotic entrees like lamb and goose. Mothers order truckloads of pizza, know that thin hamburgers are better than thick ones, and can whip up a bowl of spaghetti in a pinch.*
- Classy women *never lose their dignity. Mothers hang dignity in a closet and pull it out only for things like family photos and parent-teacher conferences.*
- Classy women *don't cry at the sight of newspaper pictures or in hospital emergency rooms. Mothers do.*
- Classy women *watch PBS specials on television while they sip tea. Mothers guard the television with a vigilant eye, and know which circuit breaker to flip if things ever get out of hand.*
- Classy women *spend their evenings in quiet conversation with friends. Mothers spend their evenings with fathers, who know that nothing sends a child off to sleep faster than the sound of parents laughing in the kitchen.*
- Classy women *don't know how to change diapers, make relief maps out of dryer lint, or untangle a child's tongue*

from orthodontia. Mothers know everything.

I don't suppose we mothers can help it. Un-classiness is simply an occupational hazard. I used to want to be a classy woman. I spent hours designing my hair, planning my wardrobe, and polishing my manners. I read all the books about dressing for success and speaking with confidence. I wanted to be a good representative of my heavenly Father and King.

But then God sent two wonderful children into my life and my priorities shifted. It became more important to raise happy, healthy, respectful children who knew and loved the God who loaned them to me.

A few summers ago I served as a counselor at middle school camp. My daughter and I joined several middle school kids for a horseback ride. As I swung into the saddle I asked the guide, "What's the name of this horse?"

The trail guide grinned. "Classy."

What a horse! Surrounded by squealing kids, horseflies, and the thick stickiness of a Florida summer, she shifted under my weight and looked back at me with a calm, forgiving eye. I leaned forward and patted her neck, then held my head high. I was as close to Classy as I ever wanted to be.

Cliques

Never will cliques be more obvious or peers more important than in the tween years. How do cliques form? Most children from families of similar social standing and wealth have similar interests, so it is natural that they gravitate toward each other. In fact, peer groups often reinforce parental values, because a child is likely to choose peers from his own social, educational, economic, and religious background. I have always been amazed at how quickly newcomers can find their appropriate peer groups.

They seem to have a special radar that enables them to find the group with which they'll feel most comfortable.

A wise parent can use peer groups. You can take your child almost anywhere as long as he takes a friend along. Want to take your tween to the theater? Tell him he can invite a friend to go along. Using the peer dynamic in a positive way can not only help you stay in touch with your kids, but also help you learn a lot about their friends.

Remember this last important insight—your tween will choose friends with whom he or she feels comfortable. If you discover that your child's best friends are involved in activities that disturb you (smoking, shoplifting, drinking, sneaking out), you'd better have a long talk with your kid. No matter how much you want to deny the possibility, there's a strong likelihood that he is involved, too—at least as a passive observer.

Clothing

Nothing can raise my blood pressure faster than a trip to my daughter's closet. Without fail, every time I open the door I know I will find perfectly good garments that my tween has never worn, some with the price tags still attached. Once, I found a darling lace dress that she had chopped in two with a pair of scissors! The price tag was still dangling from the sleeve!

I could tell that she was trying to make a skirt out of the bottom half, but she didn't know how to sew, and the hem was set with safety pins. Why didn't she ask me for help before cutting up a beautiful dress?

When I think of how much money I've wasted buying clothes that will never be worn ... well, I just want to tear my hair out. What's a mother to do?

A few tips: first, when shopping with a tween girl, make sure she tries on everything before you make your way to the cash register. That way, something that looks "dumb" when she puts it on at home will look "dumb" in the store first.

Next, when it comes to gift giving, opt for gift certificates. I gave up buying clothes for my daughter long ago. Her tastes are not my tastes, and if I pick something out, it's bound to have the stamp of "mom" on it. Tweens want to be independent, and clothing is one of the first areas in which they assert themselves.

Finally, when your child comes home and says "everyone" at school is wearing a certain item of clothing, make an effort to help your child fit in. If you can purchase only one of the specific items, be prepared to wash it several times a week. If you simply can't afford it, help your tween find a way to earn at least part of the money herself. She may decide the status symbol isn't worth it.

Some moms might feel it is wrong to allow children to mirror the clothing and styles of their peers. Granted, there are certain symbols of rebellion we don't want our children to pick up, but other things may be harmless. Is your tween's self-esteem worth an overpriced tee shirt? Only you and your child can answer that question.

Remember—children in the middle school years are comfortable when they look like everyone else. Don't make your kid be a misfit.

Commitments—Sincere and Fleeting

My friend Tracy, a fellow middle school mom, served as a camp counselor this past summer. Once school started, she felt led to begin a discipleship group for girls. She approached several girls, and the idea was enthusiastically accepted. At least ten promised they'd come to the meetings because they really wanted to learn how to walk with God.

That first night, two of the ten showed up. I saw Tracy when her first class was over, and it was hard to miss the discouragement in her eyes. "Don't feel bad and don't take it personally," I told her. "Kids of this age are very sincere when they make a promise, but they forget those promises easily. Just hang in there. You may have only three or four faithful girls, but they'll be the ones who *really* want to learn."

I'm happy to report that Tracy and her small group are doing well.

Communication

My son and I were driving home from church, so I thought I'd talk to him and see how much spiritual food he was drawing from the youth department. I glanced over at him. "What was your lesson about today, Son?"

John squirmed as if he were under examination. "I don't know."

"You don't know?" I tried not to raise my voice. "I'm sure the youth pastor talked about something. Didn't you listen?"

"Yes, I listened!" John turned to look out the window, then mumbled, "It was just the old story about Daniel and the lion's den. I've heard it a zillion times."

Oops. The doors of communication were closing, and I knew I'd have to adjust my approach if I wanted my son to keep talking. The trick, I'd learned, was to shift the attention away from John so he wouldn't feel defensive.

"I've always liked the story of Daniel," I answered, turning off the radio so we'd have silence in the car. "I've always thought that if I had half as much courage as that guy, I could handle almost anything."

I braked at a red light and waited. John said nothing, but kept staring out the window. I tapped the steering wheel and hummed softly, sending the message that I was fine, I wasn't upset, and the conversational ball was now in John's court....

"I wish I had the guts to stand up to Chip," John said, still staring out the window. "That guy makes me sick. He's always shoving the smaller guys."

I made a soft sound of sympathy, but resisted the urge to ask another question. John said something else about Chip, then moved on to rant about bullies in general, telling me more than he'd shared all week.

I pretty much remained quiet for the rest of the ride home, while John talked, his words coming faster with each passing moment. That's a nice thing about silence—it's human nature to fill it. The mother who can hold her tongue can often get her tween to loosen his.

It's easy to assume that your spouse and children know what you're thinking—and just as easy to assume you know what they're thinking. I'll never forget one Christmas when I asked Gary to help me and the kids decorate the Christmas tree. I had a picture-perfect scene in my mind—carols on the stereo, the kids happily unpacking ornaments, and me explaining the significance of each bauble as we tenderly hung it on the tree.

So, I called the kids into the living room, put the Christmas music on to play, then groaned and grunted through the artificial tree assembly. All the while, Gary was back in the bedroom watching a football game. I debated whether or not I should wait for him, but was absolutely *positive* he'd come out at any moment and join us. After all, I had mentioned my plans just that morning....

Twenty minutes went by, then thirty. The kids were restless, and I needed Gary to help me hold their attention. Nothing issued from the bedroom but the sounds of an enthusiastic football crowd.

I decided to take matters into my own hands. I dropped the box of ornaments to the floor, then strode into the garage and yanked open the door to the circuit box. There it was, clearly labeled—the breaker for the master bedroom. I flipped it, then leaned against the washing machine and crossed my arms.

I didn't have to wait long. Five minutes later Gary flew into the garage, his eyes wide. "Something happened to the power!"

"I know." I lifted a brow. "I flipped the switch."

Amazement blossomed on his face. "Whatever for?"

"Because you're supposed to be helping us decorate the Christmas tree."

If possible, he looked even more surprised. "Why didn't you call me?"

I lifted my chin. "I shouldn't have to call you. You should have *known* what I was thinking."

Ah, my fellow moms, let me be the first to tell you that fathers and daughters and sons don't know what we're thinking. Our family members may love us, but they don't know how we feel unless we explain the often-confusing emotions that trouble our hearts. And we must not be too proud to explain until we know we are clearly understood.

When you communicate something important to your tween, sometimes it's a good idea to say, "Can you tell me what I just said? Repeat it, in your own words." You may be surprised to find that what your child *heard* and what you *meant* are two totally different things. Likewise, when your child is explaining something to you, you might consider adding, "So what I hear you saying is...."

Miscommunication causes problems, so take the time to make sure you are being heard—and that you're hearing—correctly.

Confessions of a Former Wild Child

I am trying to time-travel back to my misspent youth and remember why my mother shed a lot of tears over me. It was a long time ago and I'm a different person, but I remember the feelings of confused adolescence ... oh, no!

Okay, moms. Here is the silver lining. If you are the mom of a wild child, try to remember first that he is not your child. He is God's child. God only loaned him to you, to love and train and all that good stuff until your child is old enough to do things for himself. Then, you let go and (this is the toughest part) let God. (Don't you just hate all this tough love stuff?)

When I was a wild child, I deliberately walked away from God to spend my days drinking myself half blind and partying and carousing and messing around because I thought it was fun. Hey, it WAS fun. The guy I fell in love with, moved in with, and then married—at the tender age of nineteen—was an atheist. Bummer. I wasn't a Jesus Freak, but I thought that sooner or later I'd clean up my act and get respectable and squeak into heaven at the last minute. Until then, party on, dude. I thought I was going to live forever. I knew my husband would eventually come around because, hey, he had ME to lead the way!

I drove home drunk so many times it's a wonder I'm alive. I nearly died several times from overdosing on alcohol. I broke my marriage vows. My husband did, too, so we were even. But I'm competitive, so we one-upped each other a couple more times in order to prove we were worthwhile. I considered walking away from my marriage more than once. It was boring. I wanted EXCITEMENT!

No amount of my mother's preaching made me come around. It fact, it made me mad. But I listened. I heard. I rejected it at the time, of course, because she was completely SQUARE. But I knew she was praying for me, as was my sister.

And all through my wild days, God was looking out for stubborn, wild, party-animal me. He had a plan for me way back before I knew what the plan was. My mom did what she could. She spoke Truth to me, then she prayed. (She also gained a few gray hairs in the process, but those were unnecessary because God tells us a bazillion times in the Bible, "Don't worry. I'm taking care of your little sparrow.")

For fourteen years I was married to an atheist. Our marriage had ups and downs. At year fourteen we were in the middle of trying to decide if we should get a divorce when my husband decided to go to church and talk to the pastor who'd been counseling me. He gave his life to Christ and never looked back.

Since then, God has brought us through the fire a couple more times. He's burning out those impurities. But now when we go through a crisis, he brings us through it together. We turn to him. And now our marriage is the most precious thing in the world to me. I can't envision being married to anyone more honorable, worthy, loving, and supportive. Our first baby was born on our sixteenth wedding anniversary. God's little joke, I think, sort of reaffirming our union.

So what does this windy story have to do with raising tweens? Just this: I am the sum total of all my experiences, good and bad, and I love that. I have compassion now for people who make idiotic choices, have become addicted to anything, have been afraid of everything, have divorced, lost a loved one, and been at war with God. Would I have any of those traits if I'd lived in a bubble? No.

God is watching out for your children. Your children will make mistakes that will make marvelous grownups out of them. If you are parenting a wild child, you might see your child lose *an occasional fight, but you can trust that he or she will one day win the battle. Is your own past perfectly unblemished? Probably not, and you learned from your mistakes. So will your sons and daughters.*

Don't worry about your children. Dedicate them to God. Plant seeds in their moral consciousness. They won't jump the fence into Satan's camp—at least, not for long. If your son knows the Truth, he will return to it. Perhaps, like me, he must weigh the Truth against Satan's lies. He might get beat up a little along the way, but God will be there to pick him up and dust him off.

Let God mold your daughter. God will take all the not-so-beautiful parts and turn them to his glory. Keep the faith, moms and dads, and pray. God will honor your prayers. Give your children the honest truth, then let go and love them. Accepting and loving your wild child the way Jesus would will lead him into the kingdom faster than anything else. You can trust me on this.

Conformity

I remember a cartoon I read sometime in the seventies. A bearded, longhaired, blue-jeaned peacenik stood before his father and pleaded, "But, Dad, I've *got* to be a nonconformist. How else can I be like everybody else?"

Erase the beard and change the long hair to whatever today's fashions are and you have the perfect picture of a tweenager. "But, Mom and Dad," I hear kids saying, "I've got to be different from you. How else can I find out who I am?"

So when your son sheds his childhood name, don't persist in calling Tim "Timmy." When your daughter begins to play music you detest, don't rebuke her unless it's *harmful* music. If it's merely different or not your taste, leave it alone.

The urge to look, walk, talk, and even *smell* like peers will never be stronger than during the tweenage years. Psychological studies have shown that conformity is associated with the need for acceptance, approval, and harmonious relationships with others. People who study such things have even suggested that "clothing deprivation," or not being able to dress like the rest of the group, is a real barrier in tweens' social lives. For middle school students, clothing, appearance, and acceptance by peers are so important that tweens may even look to gangs for a sense of belonging. And even gangs have a dress code.[10]

Brand names are very important at this age. You can buy your child a shirt that looks almost *exactly* like the expensive brand-name shirt his friends wear, but he won't wear the knock-off if it's the last clean garment in his closet. Kids can tell the difference, and cheaper imitations never measure up. (I know it's silly and impractical, but I'm telling it like it is.)

How can you help your child during this phase of blind adherence to the group uniform? Take him shopping ... on a budget. Give him a certain amount of money to buy his clothing for school and recreation, then stand back and bite your tongue if he decides to blow the entire amount on some ridiculously priced designer garment. Just before you reach the cash register, gently remind him that he'll have nothing left for essentials for the rest of the semester ... unless Grandma sends socks and underwear for Christmas.

Before chiding your child for brand chasing, however, look in your own closet—how brand conscious are *you*? There is nothing wrong with buying name brands that usually indicate quality, but if you refuse to wear anything that isn't a brand name ... well, you can't blame your tween for feeling the same way.

The most important thing parents can do is promote a self-esteem not based on appearance or material possessions. Praise inner qualities, not outer, even though your tween may do nothing but roll his eyes in response....

Cruelty

There's no doubt that tweens can be among the cruelest people on earth. They call each other names, they mock strangers, and they pick on anyone who is perceived as different. Writing in *Parents and Teenagers*, James Dobson says:

Junior high school students are typically brutal to one another, attacking and slashing a weak victim in much the same way a pack of northern wolves kill and devour a deformed caribou. Few events stir my righteous indignation more than seeing a vulnerable child—fresh from the hand of the Creator in the morning of his life—being taught to hate himself and despise his physical body and wish he had never been born.[11]

Why are tweens so cruel? Part of the reason lies in inexperience. They blurt out whatever thought pops into their heads, without considering the consequences. Others are cruel to their peers because tearing someone else down helps them to feel stronger. Even adults fall victim to that impulse.

Work with your tween and help him realize that everyone has feelings. The boy who's overweight, the girl who wears braces, and the boy of another race do not like being the object of ridicule, and neither would your child. Undoubtedly there have been occasions when your child has been the butt of jokes, so remind him how painful that experience was. Compassion is the act of thinking and acting kindly toward someone else, and it does not come naturally to tweens. We must teach our children to exercise it.

Dating's Rules of the Road

Hear me plainly—I don't think tweens should date. Dr. James Bray, a psychologist who teaches at the Baylor College of Medicine in Houston, says too many parents push their kids toward adulthood and dating without thinking of the consequences. "Parents see dating as cute," he says, "but they don't think that encouraging dating at a young age puts their kid out there and having to say no to sex at an even younger age."[12]

The statistics speak for themselves: The earlier a person begins to date, the more likely it is that he or she will become involved in premarital sex.

Age of Dating	Percent Who Have Sex Before High School Graduation
Twelve years	91 percent
Thirteen years	56 percent
Fourteen years	53 percent
Fifteen years	40 percent
Sixteen years	20 percent[13]

You might be able to prevent your son or daughter from dating in the tween years, but you won't be able to prevent boys and girls from discovering each other at this age. Boys who are only a few months beyond the "cootie" stage will suddenly take an interest in the young ladies around them. Girls who saw boys as best friends will suddenly grow shy and coy.

Tweenage curiosity about the opposite sex is indulged in games. Many a tween has received his first kiss during a game of "Spin the Bottle," and many an innocent young lady has been molested during "Truth or Dare." Kids fool around with things they've heard about and seen on television, but they lack wisdom. They're like underage drivers with the keys to a shiny new car, but they're not licensed, they have no experience, and they don't even know where the brakes are found. All they know is that the engine is revving, the group is cheering them on, and boy, is this ever new and exciting....

So, when the dating question arises in your home, I hope the following analogy will help you and your tween. When I teach about love, dating, and sex, I enjoy using an analogy that likens dating to driving. If you were like me, you probably did the most intense studying of your life when you were issued a study guide by your state's Department of Motor Vehicles. That thin green paperback from the DMV was easily the most popular book at my high school. We studied it, memorized it, and finally tossed our copies aside to go in and bravely take our written driver's test. We all knew how to drive, but we knew the state of Florida wouldn't give us a license if we didn't know things like how many car lengths it would take to come to a full and complete stop if traveling at fifty miles an hour.

As parents, we wouldn't let our kids drive unless they knew the rules of the road and were properly licensed. But is your tween going out with someone (though they may not be going anywhere) without knowing dating's "rules of the road"? How prepared are your kids to face "dating traffic"?

First, teach your children that *green doesn't mean "step on the gas,"* it means "proceed if the way is clear." Tell your tween that she will get a green light to begin dating when you feel she is mature and responsible enough to handle whatever might come up. Assure her that waiting is better than beginning to date through dishonesty and sneakiness. People who run red lights put themselves at great risk.

Moms and dads, let me say it again: tweens ages ten through fourteen do not need to be dating. They get plenty of social interactions at school and church. After ninth grade, some teens may be ready for group dating (several couples going out together), but you and your teenager will have to evaluate each occasion as it arises.

After mastering the green light, teach your tween that *yellow means caution*. Although most drivers speed up and rush through yellow lights, my driver's manual said yellow means "prepare to stop or proceed with caution." Is your teen in a hurry to begin dating? Does he feel pressure to have a girl-friend just because his friends are paired up? Encourage him to be cautious. Every person has his or her own timetable, and if your tween doesn't want to date, let him know you don't expect him to.

Beginning drivers should know how to *drive defensively* and make allowances for other folks on the road. As your tween begins to hang around the opposite sex, he should be "defensive," too. Even in the middle school years, girls need to know that boys are stimulated by sight; boys need to understand that a girl's revealing dress may not be intended to issue an invitation. All tweens need to be taught how to dress and behave modestly.

Do Not Pass signs are posted whenever driving is risky. Out on the open highway, passing is perfectly legal. But in danger-ous situations, drivers risk their lives by disobeying Do Not Pass signs.

Tell your tween to think of "passing" as affectionate touch. Out in the open, surrounded by friends, some light physical contact is perfectly normal between two young people who like each other. Holding hands in a crowd at a carnival is perfectly fine. Holding hands in a worship service is not. No matter how hard you try, you'll never convince me that any tween holding his girlfriend's hand is listening intently to the sermon.

Holding hands, an arm around the shoulder—there is a time and place for each of these. But there are certain risky situations where physical affection should be completely avoided. If your son finds himself with his girlfriend in a deserted classroom, a darkened hall, a parked car, or an empty house, physical affection can quickly get out of hand.

Red means STOP! A stop sign or a red light means, "Come to a full and complete stop." But *where* a driver stops is almost as important as *when* he stops. Though lines are drawn on our roads, there are no "stop lines" in dating. Teenagers often ask, "I know all the way is too far, but where along the way do we stop?"

When your teenager begins to date, teach him when to put on the brakes. When a couple first gets together, they usually hold hands. Next comes a gentle kiss, then later, more passionate kisses. Kissing usually leads to fondling, which is a warm-up for intercourse.

Clearly explain to your son or daughter that a definite caution light exists around kissing. I know godly teens who have vowed not even to kiss until after they have married. They want to be certain that their decision to marry is based upon commitment, not physical passion. For two tweens, heavy kissing and fondling are definitely *past* the stop sign.

A *Slow* sign means just that—move slowly! But too often drivers ignore the slow signs and think, "Aw, I can handle that curve...." Then, crash!

Remind your tween that her future dating years can be a delight and a discovery, but too many young people take dating too fast and end up losing control. They are then faced with an unplanned pregnancy, babies, responsibilities, and canceled dreams. Couples who wreck their dating lives wound their families, each other, and themselves.

When we *Yield* in traffic, we let oncoming cars pass us by while we wait until the road is clear and safe. It's dangerous to rush out into traffic just because everyone else is forging ahead. If your older child feels like the last virgin on earth, assure him that he will never regret waiting for the special person God intends him to marry. He will be able to present himself pure and chaste to his bride, and the journey of discovery will be a joy for them both.

Drivers who endanger the lives of others often have their licenses suspended. Gently tell your older child that if he cannot date responsibly, you may have to "suspend" his license for a while. Let your tween know that, like a driving coach, you are always available to help with dating problems. As a parent, you have valuable experiences to share. Your pastor or youth pastor may also be able to counsel your tween.

I'm not going to tell you that as parents of tweens you have nothing to worry about—I once met an eighth-grader with two babies. I've known middle school girls who were raped at parties and were too ashamed to report it; I've seen many teens get pregnant before marriage. Sexual sins are no greater than any other sin, but all sin is destructive and causes hurt. We love our kids no matter what happens, but our hearts break a little when we think of the pain that could have been avoided.

No matter what you do, when you're talking to your child about dating, assure her that you and God will always love and forgive mistakes. Even if virginity is lost or stolen, young people can make a renewed vow of chastity and keep themselves pure from that day forward.

Dessert Dividing

When two kids are squabbling over the last piece of cake or pie, your Solomon-like solution is simple: let one kid cut the dessert into two pieces, and the other gets first choice.

Discipline

Friday night I was mad enough to spit nails. Under pressure to hurry and get the house cleaned, I ventured into the guest room, which doubles as a computer/television room for our children.

I knew that my fifteen-year-old daughter, Brandi, had pretty much taken over the room, but I wasn't prepared for the mess I found. Her pencils and pens littered the bed; her bottles of nail polish and nail polish remover had been stashed beneath a desk. One section of the carpet was stained from some unknown chemical (probably the aforementioned nail polish remover); and a huge brown stain colored the throw rug (probably from a can of soda).

All these things I bore with reasonably good grace. Brandi was gone for the evening to a friend's house, so I cleaned up, muttering under my breath about the talk we'd have when she finally came home.

Then I discovered the dishes—six glasses from the kitchen, three with a skin of mold floating atop the mud-colored remains of a soft drink. In the same compartment of the computer desk I also found two plates, a knife, and two forks, and one of those single-serving trays for frozen pizza.

The dishes were the last straw. I have repeatedly told my daughter that she is not allowed to eat in the guest room, and these dishes were proof of what seemed to be flagrant disobedience. With steam rising from my ears, I gathered up the dishes and took them downstairs, then cornered my hapless hubby in the kitchen.

"We've got to do something about that girl," I said, shaking my finger in his face. "This is complete and total disregard for our house rules. It's like she doesn't care about anything but her own convenience. She just rolls her eyes at what I tell her, and look at this!" I rattled the dishes in the sink. "All of these were in the guest room. Have you thought about the roaches she's attracting?"

My poor husband blinked. "Lighten up, honey. She's a good kid."

"I know she's a good kid, but she needs to be better! She needs to obey! She needs to respect the property of others!"

My husband backed slowly away. "So, what do you want to do?"

"I'm going to put a big sign on the guest room door," I said, fuming as I opened the dishwasher. "I'm going to ban her—exile her—from that room for a month. And tomorrow, when she wants to go out with her friends, I'm going to make her pull weeds for at least a couple of hours...."

My husband made a face and backed the rest of the way out of the kitchen, probably muttering that Brandi was lucky for not being home. Mom was on the warpath.

My anger didn't fade immediately, but a couple of hours later I was feeling a little more mellow. And then the Lord brought to mind a note I had discovered in Brandi's room a year before. In a note to her best friend, Brandi had written something like, "My mom's on my case again. I think I'll go out and get pregnant."

I was sure she didn't mean it, but as I kept cleaning I discovered a new world of meaning in Brandi's words. I was so often on her case for little things like cleaning her room and returning dishes to the kitchen that she figured she ought to go out and do something major—because I couldn't possibly

harass her any more than I already was. Without know
I was fostering a "why try?" attitude in my daughter.

I felt a stab of conviction prick my heart. My daughter was
a good kid, and yet I wasn't happy ... why? Because she wasn't
perfect? I was always looking for little things to correct in her
personality ... and, heaven help me, I did "get on her case" too
much.

Right then, I asked God to forgive me ... and make me a
more understanding parent. The Lord is patient with me
when I make the same mistakes over and over again. I need
to show the same firm patience with my daughter.

When she came home the next morning, I welcomed her
back, then showed her the newly cleaned guest room. "You
know," I said, looking at her, "I want you to use this room. But
I found a stack of dishes in here last night, and you know they
belong in the kitchen. So consider yourself warned—the next
time it happens, I'll have to suspend your computer room privileges for a week. But if you'll just keep your dishes in the
kitchen, you'll have no problem."

She rolled her eyes, then retreated back into her bedroom.
That's all. There was no big miracle, no reconciliation scene,
no sudden outpouring of promises to walk the straight and
narrow path of organized tidiness.

But, I had relearned several important lessons: Don't make
huge hassles out of normal teenage problems. Warn before disciplining. Don't discipline in anger—you'll almost always
overreact. Ease up a little. I had to allow room for mistakes,
and not forget that my kid needed compliments as much as or
more than she needed discipline. We're a long way from the
finish line, but I'm pretty sure we'll make it.

When you find yourself considering discipline for your tween, first decide whether the problem was the result of flagrant rebellion or ordinary teenage antics. Do not make giant hassles out of normal adolescent problems. (See "Normal Tweenage Problems" for a complete list.)

Take a moment to think back. Did you make a mistake similar to this one when you were a tween? If so, let your memory remind you to be patient. Take a night to sleep on your thoughts and let your emotions cool.

Before approaching your tween, choose your attitude. You should discipline with the desire to teach, heal, forgive, and reconcile your child. Do not discipline to belittle, obtain revenge, or make your kid miserable.

If your child's action was an act of willful wrongdoing, discuss the situation with your spouse and resolve to respond in unity. Pray about your action. Determine to be a shepherding parent, not a vengeful, attacking, or punishing parent.

Try to determine what natural consequence should follow your child's offense ... and see if it is possible for him to experience the pain of his wrong choice. Before acting, ask yourself, "Will this heal?" If not, abandon plan A and move to plan B.

For example: If Michael is recklessly riding his bike in the street, the natural consequence might be that a car will hit him. Do you want him to experience that pain? No. Plan B might be confiscating the bike for a week. However, if Shannon is sleeping late every morning, forcing you to yell before she'll get up, warn her, then let her have her morning of sleep—and refuse to excuse her absence. Let her earn a detention and a failing grade for a missed test. The pain of her wrong choice (to stay in bed) will manifest itself.

Try to make the punishment logically fit the offense. For instance, if your child came in two hours past his curfew, make him pull weeds in the yard for two hours. You can say, "You owe me these two hours. That's how long I stayed up waiting for you."

Call your child into the room and say, "I love you and I know you have wonderful qualities even though you made a mistake. But because you have chosen to teach me that you can't be trusted (lack self-control, etc.), you have chosen for us to respond by keeping you at home (or not buying that jacket, etc.). Here's how you can teach us to trust you again in the future, and here are the positive rewards for your success: (name the conditions and rewards)." Listen to your child's response.

Finally, be supportive while your child is going through the uncomfortable consequences. Do not embarrass him publicly, and remind him it will be over soon.[14]

Drinking

Tweens and alcohol are a deadly combination. Alcohol can make a kid throw up, miss the best part of the party, or even end up dead. Alcohol causes teenagers to vegetate, regurgitate, and urinate. It can pack a hangover, put a brain to sleep, and create a drug addict—some teens become alcoholics within six months of taking their first drink. Alcohol can destroy a kid's liver, get him in trouble with the law, and hurt his heart.

Booze can interfere with teens' reproductive systems, wreck their cars, and kill their friends—more than twelve thousand young Americans are killed each year in auto accidents involving alcohol. Forty thousand more are disfigured. Alcohol can make anyone act like an idiot. It can tear a family apart. It can kill. Sure, alcohol can make a tween feel like everyone else at a party, but who wants to be like a group that is mindless, bombed, wasted, and *dumb*?[15]

If you think your tween's having a lite beer is no big deal, talk to the parents of a nineteen-year-old who has had his license suspended for drunk driving. Ask them how much they enjoy chauffeuring him to work and school; ask them about the court appearances that they've had to make on his behalf. Ask them how it feels to pick up a morning newspaper and see their son's auto accident reported on the front page.

One drink leads to another, and the earlier a young person begins drinking, the more likely he is to continue. Watch your example—and let your kids know that alcohol abuse is no laughing matter.

Embarrassed by Parents

One thing that hasn't changed much over the years is the tendency of middle schoolers to be embarrassed by their parents. I'll never forget my own middle school years—but we called it "junior high" back then. I was involved in the science program and concert choir, and whenever concert contests or science fairs came around, I was thrilled that I could travel for a day or two and be away from my parents. It wasn't that I disliked or disrespected them—it was simply great to be on my own. I was free to order what I wanted in restaurants, check into a hotel with my friends (and the chaperon lurking around the corner), and just be independent for a while.

If the concert or science fair was close enough, my parents would often drive up and join the audience for the awards presentations. I, of course, remained with my friends. I was pleased my folks cared enough to come and see me perform, but I preferred to mix with my peers.

Heartless? Now it seems so, but it didn't when I was thirteen. After all, eighth-graders are at the top of the social hierarchy. They're cool.

Loving a tween, say the authors of *The Roller-Coaster Years*, "can take on all the intrigue and secrecy of an illicit romance. The mother of an eleven-year-old boy or a fifteen-year-old girl knows what it's like to be a clandestine parent. No kisses or hugs on Main Street. No using pet names. No rendezvous in the halls at school." The protocols of a sleep-over are a particular challenge, say the authors. "You have to be there, of course, but you have to remain invisible, too, or at least out of earshot. Your role is like a downstairs maid in upstairs society: keep passing the tray of snacks, but don't intrude."[16]

Middle school students will not only withdraw from the family in public, but in private, too. Very often, except at mealtimes, you may wonder if you even have a thirteen-year-old in the house. He will be locked in the bedroom, on the telephone, or at the computer. This withdrawal is not cause for alarm; it is the foundation for the independence you'll *want* your child to have when he's twenty-five.

The Emotional Roller Coaster

My daughter came home from camp in an unusually quiet mood, and when we asked her how the week went, she burst into tears. "I want to do better," she said, sobbing. "I promised the Lord I'd spend more time in prayer and Bible study, no matter how hard it was. I made a promise never to miss a quiet time again."

We were delighted that the Spirit had convicted our daughter, but over the next few weeks of summer I noticed that she began to sleep late and spend the day in front of the television. The Bible on her nightstand remained closed. I asked her once how she was doing with her camp commitment, and she snapped her answer. "Fine."

A few weeks later, though, she decided to be honest. "I've stopped reading my Bible," she admitted. "I feel like my prayers don't go anywhere. Sometimes I wonder if God is there at all. I know I'm saved; but there are times when God just doesn't seem real to me."

I felt as though someone had plunged a dagger into my heart. How could I help her? I can't make her be spiritual. I can't make her want to love God and spend time in his word.

What's a mother to do?

First of all, mom, know that your daughter's experience is not unusual. She is sure of her salvation, and that's great. Many tweens and teens wrestle with the assurance of their salvation, especially after "mountaintop" religious experiences.

Your tween is riding the emotional roller coaster of the middle school years. Children go through an awakening in the years immediately after childhood—suddenly they are experiencing adult-sized emotions, and they don't know how to handle them. Like a cup of cold water thrown onto a hot skillet, these emotions burn and sizzle with fierce intensity and then die away. Love, hate, devotion, anger, jealousy, and happiness burn one minute and vanish the next.

I clearly remember one prayer meeting at church in my own tween years. A group of us were praying for loved ones, and several kids were weeping for unsaved relatives. I wept, too, for an uncle, and in that moment I was completely sincere and totally grief-stricken. A few moments later, however, as I rode home from church, the practical part of my brain detached from the emotional overload and wondered why I had reacted so strongly. I scarcely knew the uncle I'd been praying for, and though I was concerned about him, he wasn't especially close. But I'd been caught up in the tide of emotion and swept away in a flood of tears.

A few months ago I found three seventh-graders weeping in the girls' restroom during Sunday school. With their arms wrapped around one another, they were sobbing and incoherently mumbling about some great tragedy ... or so I thought.

I pulled Sarah out of the trio and whispered, "What's wrong?"

She sniffed and swiped at her eyes. "I don't know. I was just crying because Holly's crying."

"Fine. Now dry your eyes and go back to class."

I pulled Holly out of the other girl's embrace. "Holly," I asked, leading her toward the door. "What's wrong?"

She bit her trembling lip. "Julie's really upset."

"Okay. Dry your eyes and go back to class."

I found Julie blowing her nose into a paper towel. "Honey, are you okay?"

Sniff. "No."

I put my hand on her shoulder. "Do you want to tell me what's wrong?"

More sniffing. Then, "It's my cat. I think she might be sick."

I lifted a brow. "Have you taken her to the vet?"

"She was acting sick only this morning. But she threw up."

I nodded and tried to look wise. In as gentle a tone as I could manage, I explained that cats often vomit hairballs, grass, and any other foreign objects they manage to swallow. But if her cat was still sick the next morning, she ought to call the vet.

Julie dried her eyes and smiled. Another tragedy averted.

What causes the emotional upheaval of the tween years? Prior to adolescence a child experiences emotions as a result of *external* activities or objects—he is unhappy because certain events are bad; he feels love because people give to him; he feels excitement because an activity is fun. At the onset of adolescence, however, the tween begins to experience emotions that have their root in his *internal* being. For no reason at all, a boy or girl will feel depressed, and the tween is frequently as bewildered by the emotion as his parents are.

Girls may feel moody and blue at the time of their monthly period, and parents who ask, "What's wrong?" don't help. Tweens may not know what's wrong, they only know they don't feel happy.

Like a roller coaster, life has its ups and downs, but these are magnified during the tweenage years. Joy, pain, sorrow, and happiness—tweens delight in exploring these new emotions. They will listen to the latest hit song over and over again because it lifts them to new heights of joy or plunges them into delicious depths of melancholy. Girls devour romantic novels to enjoy exciting, vicarious love affairs, and boys experiment with drugs to experience new highs and lows.

These awakening emotions are powerful and difficult to control. Anger, rebellion, and fear can explode into physical fighting. Fits of anger often result in teary explosions during which it is impossible to reason with a tween. When you find yourself tangling with a tween in a temper tantrum, send him to his room, let the anger subside (his and yours!), then go in and try to work through the web of emotions and circumstances that caused the outburst. Tweens may not know exactly *why* they feel a certain way, so they need someone older and wiser to face these confusing emotions calmly.

Energy

The other day a middle school mom I'd never met before brought her son into our department. It was still early, so Sunday school hadn't started, and over 150 kids were talking, laughing, and playing Ping-Pong, Foosball, and pool. Music blared from the speakers, while several of the lay staff and I were checking kids in on the attendance rolls. It was mayhem—but it was *controlled* mayhem.

The new mom walked over to one of the other leaders. "Is it always like this?" she asked, her eyes wide.

Our lay staff member looked around. The kids were behaving, and the crowd was no rowdier than usual. "Yes, this is pretty normal," he said.

The woman's eyes got wider. "Do you ever have *fights?*"

Our staff member laughed. "No, thank goodness."

You may have noticed that tweens, especially boys, often have trouble controlling their bodies. Aside from the awkwardness that accompanies rapid growth, Edward Martin, who taught junior high students for several years, noticed a "general twitchiness" among his students. "Movement was the standard," he says, "tapping of hands or fingers, wiggling bodies, turning heads, bouncing, jiggling, squirming. These were not the exuberant and free movements of small children, nor the coordinated and powerful movements of youth, but rather an uncontrolled display and use of body."[17]

Mom, if your son or daughter has suddenly developed ants in his pants, it's not that he's become hyperactive overnight. It may be that he's just dealing with the extra energy that children develop in the tweenage years.

Eviction Notice

Like most mothers, I nag my son for not keeping his room clean until I sound like one of those prerecorded voices you hear on airport shuttles. One day, however, I decided to try a creative approach to the problem. There would be no yelling, no threats, no flailing of arms.

When Eric came home from school, he found the following beautifully printed notice on his door:

Because the landlord entered these premises this morning and found filth, mold, and carpet damage, the tenant who inhabits this room is hereby

Evicted

and all contents of this room

Confiscated

until further notice. Possession will be returned to tenant if the following conditions are met:

- A thorough cleaning of closet, space under bed, drawers, shelves, etc.
- Carpets shall be shampooed and scrubbed until stains are gone.
- All glasses and kitchenware are returned to kitchen and will NOT be

---

allowed back into premises. Tenant shall not use model paints or glue in this space for a full six months.

- Until the above conditions have been met, tenant is not allowed inside the room except for the purpose of cleaning.
- Any supplies needed may be brought out by a parent or found in laundry baskets. Tenant may sleep in—but shall not mess up—the guest room.

While cleaning, tenant may not listen to CD player or bring out any possessions. This room is off limits until cleaned. Landlord shall, at her discretion, begin to discard any and all items found inside these premises if room is not cleaned before October 5, 1996.

Having a room of one's own is a privilege ... and privileges can be revoked.

Respectfully yours,
The Management

I posted the eviction notice on a Wednesday morning. With church on Wednesday night, and after-school activities on Thursday and Friday, he didn't have an opportunity to clean his room until Saturday morning. Each night he slept in the spare bedroom and the next morning he pulled his school clothes from the laundry basket. (I made sure there were clean clothes available.)

On Saturday, he got up and cleaned his room! Since then I've taken to calling Saturday "National Clean Your Room Day," and when Eric is slow to crawl out of bed, I just tell him he needs to get up and celebrate a national holiday. He understands what I mean—and the consequences of not listening—without my having to nag him.

Facing Fear, Disappointment, and Bullies

When Taylor was in the fifth grade, he began to be bullied at school during physical education class. Taylor is a quiet kid, very shy and unaggressive, and it broke my heart to think anyone would pick on him. Worst of all, I could see the results in my son—he didn't want to go to school, he worried more than usual, and his usual sunny attitude completely disappeared.

We tried all the usual things—we told him to ignore the troublemakers, then we told him to tell the teacher. But the gym teacher had forty kids on the playground, and he couldn't see everything. None of the usual remedies worked.

So, feeling almost apologetic, I called the school. My call was immediately transferred into the principal's office. "We have a zero tolerance for this sort of thing," the principal said. "Hitting another child is assault and battery. We'll take care of it."

I was so impressed—she did. That afternoon I went to the school and met the two boys who had hit and bullied my son. They were sitting in the principal's office, literally spending the entire day with her. Later that week Taylor received letters from each of the boys, apologizing for how they had treated him.

I know not every situation ends as happily as that one does, but I learned a couple of things from it. First, the days of teaching our children to fight back are past. Today's schools won't excuse any sort of fighting. Second, telling my son to "just ignore the troublemakers" didn't work. And third, if it ever happens again, I'd go to his teacher or the principal immediately. No child has to suffer like Taylor did.

What is bullying? It can range from name-calling to physical assault, shoving, kicking, taunting, and teasing. It can even take the form of sexual harassment—bra snapping or teasing with sexual slurs.

"The good news," say the authors of *The Roller-Coaster Years*, "is that bullying, which often begins in third grade, wanes by high school. The bad news is that the most intense bullying occurs in middle school, peaking in the eighth grade. One study showed that as many as 58 percent of students say they skipped school once or more because they were afraid of being picked on at school by a bully."[18]

As much as we'd like to shelter our beloved children every minute of the day, we can't. You may encounter a situation where there is no principal to step in and handle the situation. So wise parents teach their tweens to cope with the unpleasant aspects of life.

If your tween makes a choice to stand up against his peer group, he may have to face ridicule, bullying, or even physical blows. This isn't right or fair. I wish I could wipe this kind of ugliness from the face of the earth, but until we get to heaven we must live in an imperfect world.

My favorite *Andy Griffith* episode is the one where Opie is bullied by a kid who demands his milk money every morning on the way to school. Andy doesn't want to embarrass his son by intervening, but he doesn't want to see Opie bullied, either.

So, Andy takes Opie fishing and tells him that when he was a little boy, he was nearly bullied out of his special fishing hole. Andy says he stood up to the bully and got a punch in the stomach as a result. But that was okay, he tells Opie, because the bully learned Andy Taylor wasn't going to back down.

The next morning Opie gathers his courage and sets out for school. A few minutes later he's back in the courthouse with Andy, wearing a bright smile and a shiny black eye. He had to take a punch, but his victory was worth the pain.

I hope your child never has to endure a bully's blow, but negative peer pressure is just as bullying an influence. "Do what we say," peer pressure says, "or you'll be sorry." Being sorry may mean being ridiculed or ostracized, so we have to help our children see that the victory is worth the temporary pain.

Family Fun

The other day my daughter wanted to paint her bedroom. I let her work on it for a few hours, then my husband and I crashed her private painting party to help her finish the job. That was the most fun the three of us have had in weeks! We laughed, flicked paint on each other, and probably got more yellow latex on our clothes than on the walls, but it was a great time we'll never forget.

Having fun as a family requires some creativity, because the last place the typical tween wants to be is out with his family on a Friday night! But in an age when both parents work and children are busier than ever with school activities, families often fracture into individuals with separate agendas.

Set aside one night—per week or per month, as often as you can—for the family. Search through idea books for fun activities and educational ventures. If the age span of your children is broad, have the kids take turns selecting a family activity.

Remember that your tween might have more fun if you choose to do something at home. Try a night making s'mores in front of the fireplace, a cookout in the backyard, or a family Monopoly tournament. Fancy family vacations are great, but the best memories are usually made at home.

Fashion

To celebrate the end of the summer one year, I took my daughter to New York. She imagines herself as sort of a fashion maven, and I'm trying to keep her feet on solid ground. We traipsed around Manhattan, window-shopped in the glitzy department stores, and bought a couple of things in off-price places.

The next weekend, when we were safely back at home, the New York Times Magazine had a Donna Karan New York ad (DKNY for the uninitiated) that featured a model wearing a white jacket made from a fitted bedsheet. I'm not kidding. The wind was blowing in the picture, and you could see the fitted elastic edge right above the inside hem.

In an effort to help my daughter see how silly fashion can be, I took the magazine upstairs and showed her that picture. "Look at this," I said, pointing to what was basically a fitted sheet with sleeves. "What do you think about that?"

She looked at it. "Well, it's very creative. I'd wear it."

"Oh, come on. So if I made you a bedsheet jacket, you'd actually go out of the house in it?"

She made a face. "Of course I wouldn't wear anything my mother made."

I rolled my eyes; she retreated back into her room. She hadn't learned the lesson I had in mind, so a few minutes later I stepped into the attic closet, plucked a lampshade off a defunct lamp, and placed it on my head. Then I knocked on my daughter's door.

"Sweetheart," I said, struggling to keep my composure as she opened the door. "I'm going to a meeting at church, so tell Dad where I've gone, okay?"

I couldn't see her face—the lampshade came down to my chin—but she took the bait.

"What," she said, her voice flat, "is that thing on your head?"

"Well," I replied airily, "since they are wearing bedsheets in New York, I figured I could certainly wear a lampshade." I lifted the shade and grinned. "High fashion, you know."

"Okay," she said, bending back over her homework. "But find another one. That one's ugly."

Sigh.

First Love

How do you handle your child's first love? I wish I could tell you just to relax and not worry, but times have changed. Kids today are so bombarded with sexual messages and images that we'd be foolish to put our heads in the sand.

When you become aware that your son or daughter is "going out with" someone (though they probably aren't actually *going* anywhere), try to talk to your child and discern what the situation is. Odds are that you'll hear about the relationship secondhand. Most first loves are a case of boy eyeing girl from across the room (or vice versa), then the Best Friend approaching the Desired One and saying, "John likes you. Will you go out with him?" The Object of Affection says yes or no, and it's a done deal ... for an hour, a week, or a month.

Your internal warning systems should go off, however, if the object of your child's affection is much older or a friend who is routinely in trouble. You may have to implement some restrictions in order to avoid encouraging inappropriate contact—don't let Susie visit Jessica's house if her "adorable" big brother will be home, for instance, and his parents will not.

Do not forbid the feelings—you might as well try to stop the ocean tides. Your child will respond, "But I can't help how I feel!" and in a sense, she'll be right. If you forbid your daughter to "like" a certain person, her feelings may shift from passion to desperate passion, an even more thrilling emotion. Remember—it's the emotion that's new and exciting. Don't invent a reason to put it in overdrive.

Gender Differences

Yesterday at lunch, Keith, one of the pastors at our church, mentioned that in just ten years his two sons (ages six and four) had done more physical damage to his house than his daughters (ages ten and thirteen) had done in twenty-three years.

"Yes, boys can be rough on a house," a mother at the table commented. "But I'll take holes in the walls and broken windows any day. Boys cause physical damage, but girls wreck your emotions."

It's often true. And fathers tend to repair the physical breaks, while mothers are often left to heal the emotional ones....

Going Out

Although the peer group is very important, older tweens also need to be accepted by the opposite sex—often by one member of the opposite sex in particular! The tweens in our area call this pairing off "going out," but all I ever get is a blank look when I ask them where they're going.

"Oh, Angie," comes the exasperated reply. "You know what we mean."

"Going out," "going together," or whatever phrase is popular in your area means that boy likes girl and girl likes boy. They are too young to date (if they have parents who enforce such things), so what do they do?

The girls whisper about the boy and smile a lot; they sit together in the back row at church. Sometimes they write notes and talk on the phone or exchange e-mail. At tween parties, they may hold hands or even kiss.

It's at this point that they bear close watching. You see,

tweens at this stage think they should do what they are expected to do, and television and the movies assure them they are expected to begin the physical rituals that eventually lead to sex. They have little emotional maturity and even less experience to tell them what *not* to do, and television and movies rarely illustrate the negative consequences to physical involvement.

We'll discuss more about this later, but if your son or daughter is just "going out" and the couple's activities are supervised, they should be fine. In most instances, going together is harmless and passes quickly. Recently one deliriously happy seventh-grade girl came up and breathlessly told me she had been going out with a boy for an entire hour!

Going together is the first taste of what is to come—a romantic relationship, the thrill of his name linked with hers, a twosome, a sometimes-togetherness. It *is* thrilling, but at the same time these fledgling romantic relationships can be a little unsettling for tweens and parents alike. Just remember that this, too, is a normal part of growing up.

Gray Areas

I'll never forget what a hard time I had dealing with my daughter about soap operas. Last summer, when I'd come home from work in the afternoons, I could tell that Megan, my thirteen-year-old daughter, had been parked in front of the television all afternoon. I don't want her to watch soap operas all day, but Megan saw nothing wrong with the sultry shows she and her friends enjoyed discussing on the telephone.

I tried saying, "Don't watch, just because I tell you not to," but that didn't work because I wasn't home to supervise the television. The temptation was too great for her to resist.

Finally, I searched the Scriptures for some answers, then called Megan into my bedroom. "Honey," I said, "I think you should be aware that everything you see or hear is stored in your subconscious mind. So, the Bible has something to say about what Christians should allow into our minds."

Together we read Psalm 101:2-4, "I will be careful to live a blameless life.... I will lead a life of integrity in my own home. I will refuse to look at anything vile and vulgar. I hate all crooked dealings; I will have nothing to do with them. I will reject perverse ideas and stay away from every evil."

I left Megan with that Scripture. I didn't forbid her to watch daytime dramas anymore; I left her feeling responsible not to me, but to the Lord. And you know what? The Lord carries a lot more weight with her than I do.

You will find that setting guidelines for gray areas is much easier if you find a scriptural principle and discuss it with your questioning tween. If your practice of "seeking and explaining" becomes a regular habit, your child will grow up with the greatest gift you could give him—the ability to use the Word of God to gain the wisdom, guidance, and comfort necessary for a complete life.

There are times when we want our children to stand for a principle because *they* believe it. For instance, if my daughter were offered a marijuana joint, I would hope she would be strong enough to stand on what *she* believes and say, "I will not harm my body. I don't believe in taking drugs," rather than refuse simply because I told her not to smoke pot.

Once a wealthy boy in our area invited nearly his entire class to his birthday party. One couple objected to their daughter's attending the party because they were relatively sure it would be unsupervised. Their daughter begged to go, though, so they took her to the party and left her with one admonition: "If anything makes you feel uncomfortable, call us. We'll come right away and pick you up."

The girl stayed at the party only ten minutes before calling her parents. The music was loud and vulgar, an R-rated movie was playing on the television, and the kissing games embarrassed her. Her parents were proud that she wanted to leave, but they were disappointed because she told the host she wasn't feeling well. Her parents wanted her to stand on her principles, but she simply wasn't strong enough to tell the truth and risk the displeasure of her peers.

That's okay—the girl left the party, and she will mature. Very few tweens are able to clearly explain their positions and principles about moral issues. Teaching—and learning—takes time.

Some principles are foundational; others are set according to parental preference. You may not want your tween to pierce his nose, for instance. There's no Scripture that expressly forbids nose piercing, but you can ask your tween to abide by your principles. Sometimes your rule can even help him save face with his peers. If my son's friends were pressuring him to pierce his nose, I'd be happy to back him up if he said I'd ground him for a year if he followed their suggestion.

On some occasions, however, you may need to rethink your parental preferences. I vividly remember being the only girl in my seventh-grade gym class who did not shave her legs. One day the other girls gathered around me and asked, "Why don't you shave your legs? Won't your mother let you?" I was stricken dumb with shame and embarrassment. When I got home, I asked my mother when I could shave my legs, and she replied, "Oh, when you're about sixteen."

My countenance must have fallen. I don't specifically remember telling her what had happened in gym class, but I do remember that she went to the grocery store and bought me a razor that same afternoon. She realized the pressure I faced, and she wisely reconsidered her parental preference.

Gross jokes

Many adults would be slightly sickened by the sight of a room in which tweens have just eaten. Any adult would be nauseated by a full dose of the gastronomical humor that comes naturally to tweens, especially tweenage boys.

This is the age when bodily functions are outrageously funny and food is meant to be not only eaten but chewed, played with, displayed, barfed, and re-eaten. To the young adolescent mind, the grossest jokes, sights, and sounds are *hilarious.*

I'll never forget the summer camp when one of our boys (I'll call him Buddy) challenged another boy to a soda-chugging match. In front of the entire camp, both boys lifted two-liter bottles of soda pop and began to gulp the carbonated drink. While the other kids stomped and cheered and whistled, Buddy won the contest and lifted his empty bottle in victory. Before he could receive his team's congratulations, however, he leaned over and upchucked every drop he had just swallowed! It sounds disgusting (and it was!), but it was one of the highlights of that year's camp. "Barfing Buddy" became a hero.

Grounding

Tweens have reached the age where grounding is a more effective discipline than spanking. What *is* grounding? It is a period of days when your child's liberty is severely restricted. All outside-the-home activities (except church and school) are eliminated, as well as in-home entertainments (TV, movies on the VCR, computer games, the telephone). If you ground a child by forcing her to stay in her room, where all the modern conveniences are available ... well, she's not feeling too inconvenienced, is she? The point of discipline, and of grounding, is to create a level of discomfort that the child will not want to repeat while not doing irreparable harm to body, soul, or spirit.

The following are some tips to insure that grounding is an effective discipline:

Keep your word. If you've promised Zack that he'll be grounded the next time he leaves without telling you where he's going, follow through. Don't accept a flimsy excuse, and don't let him make you feel guilty.

Make sure you can enforce your terms. If you stipulate that Heather may not watch television for a week, make sure she cannot watch television. Either be home to make sure she can't, or flip the circuit breaker. If you don't put action behind your words, you may be subtly encouraging your child to cheat.

Make the rules clear. Does this grounding mean no television? No telephone? No computer games? No Nintendo? No going to Grandma's? No visiting the neighbors? If this particular grounding means that your child will miss an extra-special event, you and your spouse should decide beforehand whether or not the event will be considered an exception or a lost opportunity.

Set a time limit. I've heard kids say their parents were so angry that they were "grounded for life." That punishment isn't effective, because your child knows you don't really mean it. On the other hand, I've heard of kids being grounded for an entire *year* ... and parents enforcing it.

Make the grounding relate to the offense. If your child has broken a family Internet rule, for instance, for a certain period of time you can disconnect the Internet or change the access password. If your child has broken curfew, you might institute an earlier curfew for six months. If your teenage son fails to fill the gas tank, you can take away his car keys for a month. Not every offense has to result in solitary confinement with every privilege taken away.

Before you institute the grounding, have a calm and rational discussion with your tween about the offense and the resulting discipline. Ask your child what he would do if he were in your position. Be very specific about what you expect in behavior, during the grounding and afterward.

Reward and praise your tween when she does well. When your daughter remembers to call and tell you where she is, thank her for her consideration. When your son brings up that D in history, make cookies to celebrate. Let your child know that you appreciate the things he does right.

Be willing to offer "time off for good behavior." Another mom says: "If our kids seemed truly repentant and took their punishment without complaining; and *especially* if they volunteered to do dishes or laundry or extra cleaning while they were grounded, we were more than happy to take a few hours or days off their penalty. This was especially helpful when our kids' grounding had, in effect, grounded *us* as well."

Be consistent. This last suggestion is probably the hardest to enforce. It's so easy to let misbehaviors slide when we're tired, distracted, or busy, hoping for the best from our children. But if a behavior is not acceptable on Monday, it should not be ignored on Tuesday.

Growing Up Too Fast

The other day I was looking at the family computer where my daughter has been working on a school project. I found a stack of old papers and was about to throw them out, but I saw that she had made a list of passwords for her Internet e-mail accounts. Her password on every account was "lose20lbs."

I was heartbroken. She is a beautiful fourteen-year-old, and exactly the right weight for her height. If she lost twenty pounds she'd look sick ... and would probably be anorexic.

I spent the rest of the day searching through my life to see if my own preoccupation with dieting had somehow influenced her. I don't know, but I don't think so. I really could stand to lose more than twenty pounds, but I don't often talk about diets in front of my daughter.

I suppose it's a combination of things—the stick-thin models in magazines she reads, the size two actresses on her favorite television shows, and our national obsession with youth and attractiveness. Have we BOTH been brainwashed by the world?

I just hate to see my beautiful girl worrying about such things in her teens. She's not even finished growing, and already she's unhappy with how she looks. She's just growing up too fast.

Ten years ago, when parents told their misbehaving tweens, "Act your age," it meant that they wanted their children to drop the babyish and immature behavior. Today, if a parent were to tell his tween to act her age, it might mean, "Don't be in such a hurry to grow up."

By age twelve, the words children now use to describe themselves in focus groups include "flirtatious, sexy, trendy, cool." Fifty years ago, says *Newsweek*, when girls talked of self-improvement, they meant helping their neighbors or improving their grades. In adolescent girls' private diaries and journals these days the body is a consistent preoccupation, second only to peer relationships.[19]

Tweens no longer play with toys. The Toy Manufacturers Association reports the audience for toys now tops out at age ten, not fourteen.[20] So, if you're thinking about getting your eleven-year-old a toy robot for his birthday, better think again.

Instead of toys, most tweens today could use an electronic organizer. Many tweens today are scheduled to the max. With school, piano lessons, gymnastics, tennis, sports teams, plus church activities, they are constantly on the go, as busy or even busier than their parents. Gone are the carefree days of childhood.

"Girls are having more trouble now than they were thirty years ago," writes psychologist Mary Pipher in her book *Reviving Ophelia*. "The protected place in space and time that we once called childhood has grown shorter."[21]

The fractured family also plays an important role in the early maturation of tweens. Psychologist Pat Hudson says divorce can be a major factor in kids' acting like adults before they can legally obtain a driver's license. "When I first started doing therapy," says Dr. Hudson, "I saw a lot of runaway kids. Now I hardly see any. Now I see a lot of throwaway kids, where a parent just drops out of their lives. Things didn't work out ... so, 'Sorry, kid.'"[22]

Gary and I have noticed this in our own youth department. Kids who were formerly carefree become serious and silent when their parents are in the throes of a divorce. And afterward, when a young person is busy looking after his wounded custodial parent, the roles of caregiver and dependent are often reversed. Maturation arrives quickly, and at a terrible price.

Television also plays a role in the quick disappearance of

childhood. While we grew up watching the *Partridge Family* and the *Brady Bunch*, today's tweens are watching *Dawson's Creek* and *South Park*.

How can parents keep kids from growing up too fast? It may be impossible in today's society, but there are ways to keep the parent-child bond in place. For instance, parents might consider ways they can work at home. We're fortunate, because a writer can work practically anywhere, and youth pastors have fairly flexible hours. We've been able to insure that our children can reach us anytime they need to—though I'll admit that the temptation to "zone out" when I'm working is still strong.

In an article in the *Washington Times*, writer Suzanne Fields mentioned one mother, a full-time marketing manager, who reduced her work to three days per week when her daughter turned fourteen. She took a 40 percent pay cut for "100 percent more interaction," but said the emotional payoff was priceless.[23]

It's not only the kids who benefit when one or both parents rearrange their lives. Most adults like working at home. I love the flexibility, the ability to be home for repairmen and UPS deliveries, and the freedom to work at night if the morning is crowded by other obligations. Many office workers, from insurance salesmen to marketers, are finding that hours spent in a home office can be more productive than those spent in an office complex. Technology has made it possible to accomplish almost anything from a home office. If you're self-motivated, there are fewer distractions and greater emotional rewards, which makes for happier employers and employees.

If a home office is feasible, moms and dads, you might consider it!

Hair ...To Grow or Not to Grow

*When the "skater" haircut was popular, each of my four sons
and all their friends wore that style even though none of them
were skaters. (To refresh your memory, the skater cut was long,
straight hair from the crown to the top of the ears, then short
layers underneath. It's sometimes called a bowl cut.)*

*A mutation of this style developed, and Daniel, one of my
sons, had a "shaved under" haircut—hair parted down the
middle and long from the crown to the chin, with the under-
layers shaved away. I didn't care for this style at all, but I said
nothing. He told me the girls liked his hair like that! I thought
he looked like a romance novel cover model....*

*Though I cringed every time I looked at his hair, I never
demanded that he cut that mess. I wanted him to change it, I
prayed he would see the light, but for the many months he wore
this style I kept my mouth shut. Finally, much to my relief, he got
a normal haircut and discovered that the girls still liked him.
He also learned that he could make a style change without
affecting his "coolness" level. I learned that God answers
prayer! (I knew that, of course, but it was a pleasure to be
reminded.)*

*I think our job as parents is to train up our kids in the way
they should go. I praise God that each of our sons has made a
decision for Christ. We didn't need the great hair debate to put
a wedge between us during the important middle school years.*

*I don't think Jesus was overly concerned about appearance
when he walked the earth. He looked at the state of each heart,
and he wasn't fooled by fancy clothes or distracted by goofy hair-
cuts. Until a young person matures enough to realize that it's*

what's on the inside that counts, a fashionable haircut can go a long way.

As the mom of four boys, I've learned to choose my battles wisely. There are so many more important things than hairstyle. Our sons know that their father and I are their number-one fans, and we support them. We hope they will come to us with their problems. So far, each of them has survived middle school and their hair looks great!

Hero Worship

I'll never forget one Sunday morning several years ago. A musical drama team came in to do an improvisational performance, and someone mentioned the name of Michael Jackson, who was then at the peak of his popularity (now I'm really dating myself!).

The name started a buzzing among the girls in the front section. "You hush up about Michael!" one girl shouted, while a pair of others got up and huffed out of the room.

Strong hero worship is a trait of middle school students. Your child may idolize the latest pop group, an athlete, or even a teacher at school. This is fine; it's perfectly normal that our children shift their attention from us to other adults. Our challenge lies in demonstrating that the quiet neighbor who volunteers to come over and repair a broken pipe is probably more deserving of praise than the sports hero who makes four million a year, looks good on TV, and abuses drugs.

A tip: since we live in a media-saturated culture, be on the lookout for celebrities who truly honor Christ. Save newspaper and magazine clippings about athletes with dynamic testimonies, and call your children to the television when the news features a man who thanks God for giving him the strength to pull people from a burning building. People—especially tweens—are more drawn to glitz than to genuine selflessness, so take the time and make an effort to point out people and actions worthy of praise.

There's a man in our town who has blessed our family beyond words. His name is Bill W. (I'd include his last name, but I'm afraid the man's phone would begin to ring nonstop). Bill is the father of ten children, grandfather to twenty-five and counting, and retired from the FAA. But he doesn't rest on his laurels or kick back for a well-deserved rest. Instead he counts his retirement years as a time for the ministry of service. If he's not taking care of his wife's aging mother, he's volunteering at the church's thrift store or repairing a college student's car. And if he's not busy with one of those things, he's usually at our home, repairing something that Gary and I can't fix (which is just about everything in the house).

Bill has retrieved rats from our attic, chopped down tree limbs, and climbed on the roof to replace an attic fan. He once rode three miles on a riding mower along a busy highway—the easiest way to get it from his house to ours. He never asks a penny for his work, and always protests loudly when we force a gift certificate or other token of appreciation into his hand. He sees his volunteering as a service of gratitude for the Lord. Bill is a true hero, the kind of man I want my kids to idolize.

My husband told me that the other day he and my son were pulling into the driveway when they saw Bill's car parked by the fence—he had come over to look at a faulty breaker in my circuit box. Without any prodding, my son turned to my husband and said, "You know, Bill is a good man."

I can't write this without tears in my eyes. A true hero has entered our lives, and my kid had enough discernment to recognize him.

Thank you, Lord.

Homesickness

My two tweenage daughters, Kristen and Laura, went off to camp for a week. Kristen, the older girl, loved every minute. Laura, who had not been able to join in the camp activities with the same enthusiasm as her sister, cried herself to sleep every night and was thrilled to be back home.

I had to admit that Laura's homesickness was flattering. I was relieved that Laura missed us and half-annoyed that Kristen didn't.

But my husband understood our daughters' behaviors: "Kristen is more responsible and more ready to be independent," he told me. "She has had more opportunities to grow up and is closer to being the strong Christian woman we'd like her to be someday. It isn't bad that Laura was homesick; we just need to realize that the girls are far apart in development."

He's right, of course. Just because two children come from the same parents doesn't mean they'll be alike.

Keep Those Hugs Comin'

When our two boys thought they were too old for real live hugs, we found that a friendly wrestling match was a great stand-in! Just beware of that awkward stage when your young man doesn't realize his brute strength, or you might come out of those "hugs" black and blue!

Although the tween years are a time of pulling away from parents—often literally—keep giving those hugs of approval and affection. Just don't hug your son in front of his friends.

Let your tween set the boundaries for physical contact. A self-conscious middle schooler will not be as eager to receive hugs and kisses as the four-year-old you once knew, but it's not necessary to avoid all physical affection. Respect your child's limits, all the while assuring him of your faithful support and love.

Identity. Who Am I Today?

In the sixth grade, I was known as Angela Elwell. I wore my hair short and pulled tightly to one side of my head with a barrette. I had a severe overbite and was the only one in my class who wore ankle socks with tennis shoes. I made straight A's and favored the library over outdoor activities. My teachers were my best friends. I remember once asking the librarian for a book on child psychology, and though I can't remember why I asked, I'll never forget the look of puzzlement on her face.

In the seventh grade I asked people to call me "Angie" and changed the way I wrote cursive "t's" at the end of words. I found two best friends; we became a threesome. I loosened up—the ankle socks and the barrette disappeared, and some B's began to appear on my report card. Braces took care of the buck teeth. I stopped wearing my cousin's hand-me-downs (I outgrew her) and started sewing my own clothes. I went through an animal-loving phase, so my mom had to cope with breeding gerbils, two baby chicks, kittens, a dog, a parakeet, and my intense desire for baby rabbits. (I never got the rabbits. My mom had her limits.)

Today I still cross my "t's" the way I chose to in the seventh grade. My close friends still call me Angie. And my house is home to three dogs, two cats, and a rabbit—even though I'm allergic to them. The changes I consciously made in the seventh grade have, for the most part, remained.

Your child, too, will begin to adjust certain aspects of his identity. He will shuck off the persona you have given him as easily as he discards the clothes you buy. Some of these passing phases will be incorporated into the person he will ultimately become; others will fade away. Tweens "try on" different identities to see which ones suit them best.

Along with this search for a genuine identity comes the accompanying fear that the person inside will not measure up to the accepted standard, whatever "accepted" is. Each tween wrestles with two sets of characteristics: an unchangeable physical set (hair and eye color, body size, facial features, etc.), and a much larger intangible set which can only be defined by comparison with his peers. Is your child intelligent? Athletic? Confident? Popular? Pretty? Your tween will determine how many of these qualities she possesses by comparing herself with others.

Comparison—ah, and therein lies the pain. Some days your tween will feel like he's on top, at other times he will consider himself at the bottom of the heap. Let him know that at home, at least, he is loved for who he is and compared to no one else— not even a sibling. Most of all, remind your child that her identity and worth are rooted in Christ, not in the world's standards. We are loved, we are *important*, because Jesus Christ loved us enough to give his life for us.

Last year I bumped into a young man whom I'd known in middle school as Franklin McConnell. I discovered that he was now "Thomas McConnell"—he had decided to use his middle name as his given name. I smiled, said, "Hello, Thomas," and made a mental note to adjust my thinking. In my mind he will always be "*Franklin* Thomas McConnell," but I hope to remember to use his new name.

Inappropriate Infatuation

I'll never forget the first time I felt the overwhelming rush of love. I was in fifth grade and totally enamored with a dashing character on television. He was handsome, brave, courageous, virtuous ... everything a man should be. I was only a *little* disappointed by the fact that he was a cartoon.

As tweens seek new adult influences, boys and girls sometimes develop passionate emotional attachments to older women and men. Though boys do not often develop a crush on an older woman (and when they do, rarely do they do anything about it other than daydream), most girls go through at least one mad crush on an older male figure.

My husband and I have noticed that girls who have no father in the home or who have an "absentee" father are especially prone to developing crushes on movie stars, teachers, or older teenage boys. Parents who are concerned about these intense "affairs of the heart" can rest assured that they are harmless—unless unnaturally encouraged. Tweens are just learning about the rush of feeling that we call "love," and they are in love with the emotion more than anything else.

I am very aware of how alarming this situation can be. I've read magazine and newspaper articles about adults—males and females—who took advantage of this age's susceptibility to hero worship and seduced children. I would never tell you to shrug off what may or may not be a harmless infatuation.

After you know with whom your daughter or son is infatuated, judge whether this person can be trusted around your naïve youngster. If this adult is responsible, don't worry, but do continue to be cautious. If he or she is an adult with whom you are not acquainted, you would not be out of line to drop in and say, "My son thinks a great deal of you and I just wanted to meet you."

Make sure your child isn't spending unreasonable amounts of time with this person, and try to make sure they are not spending unsupervised time alone. Never assume anyone is harmless. Even youth pastors and teachers who may need to privately counsel your tween should have other people around.

If the infatuation amounts to nothing but "sighing from afar," let it go and don't worry. It's a phase that's usually harmless.

The Internet—We're Wired Now!

A few months ago I read a magazine article that explained how we can discover which web pages our family computer has visited in the past several days. When I opened these files, I discovered that several of the web pages stored on my computer were pornographic sites.

I was shocked beyond words. The only people who use the computer are myself and my son, and I hardly ever visit anything on the web but a few shopping sites. So this meant that my thirteen-year-old son had to be the one who had visited these vile web pages....

I talked to him, and at first he denied everything. But then, when I showed him the proof, he broke down and confessed. He had been curious, he said, and once he started looking, one page led to another....

Since that day we've instituted some safeguards on the family computer because I know pornography is addictive. These things weren't an issue when I was growing up, but times certainly have changed. Now we keep the computer in the family room, where everyone can see what's on the screen, and we check the files occasionally to see where our computer has been....

Times *have* changed, moms and dads, so when you think your tween is upstairs doing his homework, he may be in the company of a pornographer or a pedophile via the Internet. In a day of instant access and chat rooms, you cannot be too careful.

How to discover where your computer's been hanging out: Even if you're not terribly computer literate, you can discover which web pages your computer users have been visiting.

For instance, if you are using Windows 95 or 98, first open the program called *Windows Explorer*. You will see the screen filled with two frames, one on the left side and one on the right. The left side column contains all the folders on your "C" drive—usually your computer's main hard drive. Scroll down until you see *Windows* (the folders are listed in alphabetical order). There is a tiny plus sign in a box immediately to the left of the word *Windows*. Click on the plus sign.

Now you will see a long list of all the file folders inside the *Windows* folder. Look down the list until you see *History*. Click on the plus sign beside *History*.

Next you will see another series of folders—a folder for *Last Week*, and a folder for every day of the week since. By clicking on the plus sign beside any of these folders, a list of web sites will drop down. By clicking on any individual web sites, another list will appear in the frame to the right of the screen—these are the actual URLs (addresses) of the web pages your computer has visited. By double-clicking on any of these URLs, your computer will open the page and display it without going online. (For at least a week, depending upon your computer settings, these pages are stored on your hard drive, in case you want to visit them again).

I firmly believe that every parent with a computer in the home should visit the History folder every couple of weeks just to be certain his or her children aren't stumbling onto bad sites. In addition, there are many wonderful computer programs that screen out objectionable material so children are not exposed. One of my favorites is CyberPatrol, which not only refuses to let a computer visit a pornographic page, but it also limits the number of hours a child may spend surfing the Internet each week. In addition, it will not allow a child to type certain words in e-mail or "instant messages." For instance, if you wanted to prevent your daughter from giving out her phone number, you would type the phone number into the forbidden word list. If she tried to type it, the screen would read XXX-XXXX.

For more information about CyberPatrol, visit www.cyberpatrol.com. A free trial version is available and can be downloaded from the web. The list of inappropriate sites is regularly updated, so, once the program is installed, you should make sure to check for updates.

The Internet can be a burden and a blessing. I've used it for everything from buying a car to treating migraines, but technology also brings its share of frustration. E-mail is wonderful, and can place you in touch with people you would never take the time to call, but it also spawns rumors, junk mail, and impulsive reactions.

In our household, we've implemented three guidelines for Internet use:

1. No giving out our name or address online.
2. No talking to strangers.
3. Absolutely no chat rooms, not even those designated for teens. Sexual predators have been known to disguise themselves and hang out in chat areas.

The jury is still out on instant messaging programs such as ICQ and AOL's Instant Messenger. These are a pain (you have to stop what you're doing to chat), and these programs can make it easy for a stranger to initiate a conversation with your child. There are ways to block messages, but even though the kids love being able to communicate instantly with their friends, the process makes me nervous. Use these with caution, and set up safeguards.

Just Say No

It's a simple word, short and sweet. Two lovely sounds, an N and a long O, blended together. Nooooo.

Not long ago I received an e-mail from a friend who was concerned because her teenage son wanted to attend a Marilyn Manson concert. "Please join me in praying that the concert is cancelled," she wrote. "I'm so disturbed I don't know what to do."

All together now—take a deep breath, position your tongue against the roof of your mouth, and say that simple word: "No."

Too many parents avoid this word like an animal avoids a fire. I know it's not fun to say "No," especially when your tweens have their hearts set on something. But you're the *parent*. And parenting involves saying "No" to anything that might harm your child.

You don't want to go around saying "No," to every request—say it too much, and it loses its power. If you forbid even reasonable requests, your children might develop a "what's the use?" attitude and begin to disobey behind your back. But when it comes to truly important issues, especially those that might put your child in harm's way, just say "No."

God's not shy about saying "*No.*" The Ten Commandments, which psychologists and theologians alike regard as a blueprint for a well-ordered society, are a veritable list of no's. No worshipping other gods. No idols. No misusing the name of God. No desecrating the Sabbath. No disrespecting your parents. No murder. No adultery. No stealing. No testifying falsely. No coveting your neighbor's possessions.

Why, then, are some parents so shy about using the word?

Are we afraid our children won't like us? Are we afraid we'll drive them into rebellion? Moms and dads, if hearing *"No"* makes your child throw a fit, he's already *in* rebellion. He's doing what he wants to do while you're throwing open the door and inviting him to go his own way.

My parents said "No" to two young men I had promised to marry. The first was a fine young Christian man who proposed to me just before my seventeenth birthday. I went into the house with a ring on my finger and calmly told my parents that I loved my boyfriend and had promised to marry him. We'd wait a year, at least until I was eighteen, and then we'd live happily ever after.

My parents thought and prayed about it for a few days, then they called me into the living room and told me "No." They were convinced that this young man was not God's will for my life.

Did I accept this without a quarrel? Of course not. I wept and wailed and gnashed my teeth, but then I realized that if I wanted God to bless my life, I had to respect and honor my parents. After all, that was God's command. So I gave the ring back and broke off the engagement.

Yes, I suppose I could have suggested eloping ... or any number of desperate things. But my parents had raised me to know right from wrong, and I wanted my marriage to be *right*.

A year later I was dating another wonderful young Christian man. After going together a long time, he proposed, and I agreed to marry him. We told my parents, who thought and prayed about it, then came back to tell me they were convinced this young man was not God's will for my life.

Once again, I wept and wailed. I was traveling full-time with a musical ensemble, away from home, but I knew the principle of parental authority had not changed. So even though it broke my heart (which proved to be pretty resilient), I wrote one of the hardest letters I've ever had to write and broke off the engagement.

Three years later, I met Gary. He proposed, and I called my parents and gave them the news. They thought and prayed about it, then told me I had their blessing.

Whew.

Moms and dads, if you feel strongly about something, that insistent feeling may be the Spirit of God warning you. Don't be afraid to tell your child "No." Let them wail and whine and gnash their teeth—when the emotional outburst is finished, they'll respect you for your wisdom, particularly if you act in their best interest.

Keep Your Marriage Strong

Twenty-five years ago when Gary and I began working in youth ministry, most of our counseling with kids centered around peer problems and identity issues. Today we spend most of our time dealing with fractured families and brokenhearted kids.

Adolescence is difficult enough without battling the grief and guilt of a broken home. No matter how amicable a divorce may be, psychologists have noted that nearly all children see themselves as the reason for the family breakup. Unfortunately, most children enter the tween years at the same time their parents are entering midlife, with all its attendant crises and reevaluations.

Please, moms and dads, take the time to keep your marriage strong. Spend quiet time alone with your spouse and recapture the romance of your marriage. Show by example how a Christian man and woman conduct themselves lovingly and respectfully in a marriage ordained by God. Your example may be the best reason your child will have for maintaining high moral standards when he or she begins to date and seek a life partner.

Take a few moments sometime to talk with your tween about marriage. By casually asking, "What sort of person do you want to marry?" and continuing the discussion, you can begin to instill the values your child will need for a solid foundation when he or she begins to seriously consider marriage.

One word of warning—don't talk about marriage *too* much. I used to tell my daughter that she needed to know how to clean house and shop and cook because she'd need to know these things when she got married, then I discovered that she felt I was pressuring her to date and get married! I immediately dropped all references to hope chests and housekeeping. Now when I urge her to get in the kitchen, I talk about skills she'll need for her after-college apartment.

If yours is a blended family and divorce is already part of the family picture, be honest with your children and try your best to do these two things: (1) Give your child the freedom to love his other parent, and (2) never criticize the other parent. Your child feels that he or she is a part of both of you, and if you criticize your child's other parent, you are, in effect, criticizing your child.

Label Makers

Where would we be without labels? If you were to step into your pantry and prepare dinner from a collection of unlabeled cans and packages, you'd probably end up with an interesting but unappetizing meal.

Like those cans on your pantry shelf, tweens are labeled by peers, family, church workers, teachers, even physicians. Human nature tends to simplify by lumping groups of people together and ascribing certain characteristics to the entire group. Entire generations of prejudice have been based upon such assumptions.

Ask your child, and odds are that he'll be able to identify the class clown, the brain, the athlete, the bully, the princess, and the outcast. Teachers speak of their students as "ADD, LD, or EH," and parents echo those phrases. Labels are often applied thoughtlessly, and a child never realizes that he or she can outgrow or outperform a negative label.

Labels have surprising staying power. I remember the boy who was labeled our class "brain" in the sixth grade. He was bright, but we were all surprised when someone else proved to be our class valedictorian in the twelfth grade.

When I took my first teaching job I replaced a teacher who had left two weeks into the school year. I didn't know a thing about my students, and I graded their first essays with a strict and impartial eye. When I handed Andrea's paper back to her, she turned pale. You see, I learned later that Andrea was the class "brain," and no teacher had ever given her less than a 95, while I gave her a 93! She spent an hour after class with me, thoroughly probing my grading system so she would never fall short again.

How can you help your child avoid being branded with a label? Here are ten little things you can do to help your child discover his true self:

1) Don't make negative predictions about your child's future. Avoid making comments such as, "You're just no good at math," or, "You're like me—a klutz when it comes to sports." We have to remind ourselves that God has a unique plan for each of our kids. We don't know what God will do in the future. Young minds do awaken, and young bodies do bloom into maturity.

2) Expose your tweens to healthy adult role models of all sorts. Make certain your child knows someone in a wheelchair, an adult who would have been diagnosed with ADD, a successful businesswoman *and* a happy stay-at-home mom. Show your child that nothing is impossible with God's blessing and hard work.

3) Help your tween explore his unique interests and talents, and don't assume those interests and talents will mirror your own. If she's musical, invest in an instrument. If he's athletic, sign him up for a sports team. But be prepared for a flagging of interest. It's a good idea to ask your child to finish his term of commitment—the semester or the season—but if she hates softball, don't sign her up for a second year. If she's truly athletic, and you want to encourage her natural ability, ask if she'd be interested in soccer instead.

4) Give honest approval for a job well done. Honest praise means more to your child than she will let you know.

5) Frequently ask yourself what you expect—and if that expectation is realistic. Be aware that without realizing it you may be prejudiced about what your child can and cannot do. You may

want your beautiful daughter to model in New York, but if she's five foot two, you should reconsider. You may want a son who'll play professional sports, but if he has a non-competitive, easy-going personality, it may never happen.

6) If your child has been diagnosed with ADD, learning disabilities, or some other medical condition, don't reinforce prejudices. Don't refer to your child's learning disability in every conversation with teachers—especially in your tween's presence. Don't announce that your daughter is hyperactive in front of the cousins at Thanksgiving dinner. Don't be quick to ascribe your son's short attention span to ADD—it may be just an ordinary juvenile attention span. (I've noticed that *I* have a short attention span these days. If I'm not absolutely riveted by something, I'm ready to move on to something else. I honestly think television and the fast pace of life have affected all of us). Share medical information only with those who need to know.

7) Remember that children are different, and they all pass through stages. You don't have a "quiet child" or a "boisterous child," you have a child who is often quiet or one who is often active. Try saying, "You're in a talkative mood," instead of "You're a big mouth." Don't apply a negative label—it just might stick.

8) Use the power of labels in a positive way. When my daughter was young, my husband called her "sweetness." That'd be a good habit to pick up again....

9) Don't compare siblings to one another. It's so easy to say, "Oh, Jane got the brains, and Todd got the athletic ability." You can congratulate Jane on her excellent report card and Todd on his touchdowns, but give Jane room to play ball and Todd a chance to make A's.

10) One night when your family is together and the mood is relaxed, tell your children about the labels you wore, growing up. Hearing that their dignified dad once struggled with the nickname "Squeaky" will help the kids realize that they *will* eventually mature.

Lead Your Child to Christ at an Early Age

I'm grateful to my parents for many things, but chief among them is the fact that I accepted Christ at age six. I clearly remember going to Vacation Bible School and seeing a puppet presentation that illustrated how people deserve punishment for sin, but Jesus stepped in and took the punishment for us. At home I asked my mother about accepting Jesus as my Savior, and that night I prayed to receive Christ.

In order to be sure I understood what I had done, my parents wanted me to wait a year before being baptized, but children of seven and eight are able to understand spiritual conditions and make a commitment to their faith. Statistics indicate that relatively few people make a commitment to Christ after age twelve, and the odds against a salvation decision grow greater with each passing year.

Several years ago I interviewed Dr. Clyde Narramore, a pioneer in the field of Christian psychology. He told me that one of the best ways parents can love their children is to lead a child to the Lord at an early age:

Help him understand that God is the Creator of all things. Lead him in paths of righteousness. Explain everything in spiritual terms as much as possible. Say, "Look at that tree. It's continually pumping water to its many parts. There's a wonderful pumping system inside the tree. Do you know who put it there? The Lord did."

Really, it doesn't take an awful lot of maturity to realize that you've done things that are wrong, that sin displeases God, and that God sent Jesus Christ to die for us. Children can use computers at three and four. They can know and do much by the time they are five. Consequently, they can understand the gospel at a very young age.

I think it may be detrimental to a person's intellect if he has to live in this world and not understand many basic concepts such as sin, salvation, Christian growth, and God's working throughout the world.[24]

Moms, don't think your child has to be eighteen before he can choose his spiritual destiny. Your tween certainly has the capability to understand spiritual things and receive Christ *right now*. Rich spiritual knowledge can give your child wisdom beyond his years and help him persevere through many difficult situations.

Don't let your tweens go through the adolescent years spiritually unprepared. Lead them to spiritual truths, or find someone who can.

Learning to Let Go

As your child enters the tween and then the teen years, your role will change from parent-manager to parent-consultant. Teens want to feel they are controlling their own lives ... and that you are available for input and guidance. As the parents of tweens and teens, you don't have a lot of control over your kids. You can say "No," but they won't automatically obey. What you *do* have is influence, so use it wisely.

When your child entered your family, you held him in your arms and glowed with happiness as an appreciative audience of friends and relatives applauded. When he took his first steps, you stood by his side and held his hands. As he learned and grew, you were there, guiding his hands, training his mind, shaping his life. When the audience grew smaller and no one else applauded, you and your spouse stomped, whistled, and clapped like mad for this kid you adore.

Now your child is older, and he is ready for you to stand in the wings as he faces his public. Your guidance and discipline are still sorely needed because he is unsure of the limits of the stage and he needs your protection. But as he grows older, little by little he will find his own way and test his own limits. Your guidance and protection will be needed less and less often, but take heart. Your support, love, and wisdom will always be appreciated.

Your son or daughter, even when an adult, will still need an approving audience.

Makeup

Black nail polish, eyelid glitter, scented lip gloss—these are just a few of the outrageous products tween girls love. Bizarre colors and vulgar exaggeration fit right into tween extremes. Domestic sales of makeup for preteens are estimated to run as high as $200 million—a profitable share of the $3 billion mass-market cosmetic business.[25]

Our middle school department has an annual September ritual—an immodest fashion show, in which our female lay leaders go far beyond the call of duty and dress to exaggerate certain immodest traits. One of our characters is "Molly Makeup," and this is a bit of her introduction:

> When Molly Makeup turned thirteen,
> She realized her fondest dream.
> "You can wear makeup," her mother said,
> But Molly's freedom went to her head!

Tween girls don't always understand that the natural look is beautiful, so, sometimes they get carried away! Help your daughter avoid the "painted face" look by suggesting that she use natural colors (yes, clear mascara and lip gloss are available) and reserve the bizarre stuff for slumber parties and costumes.

"Mama's Boy"

The greatest fear of a middle school boy is to be known as a "mama's boy" or a crybaby. Crybabies and mama's boys have a rough time of it because they aren't accepted by boys who have established their independence and social status. They aren't cool.

Unfortunately for boys who are sensitive, physically small, easily embarrassed, or shy about leaving the protection of home, the situation is made worse by the self-appointed bully who exists in nearly every tween group.

What creates a bully? The desire for social acceptance and status. What makes a shy kid keep coming back for continued harassment? The same desire for acceptance.

I'll never forget the year Bill was in our middle school department. At twelve years old, Bill was six feet tall and weighed 180 pounds. He was a Christian and a very likeable boy in the company of adults, but an impossible bully with the younger kids. He wasn't malicious like some bullies are, but when a smaller boy entered the room, Bill could never resist the urge to walk over and playfully punch the smaller boy in the stomach or slap him hard between the shoulder blades. He pulled his punches—a little—but the force he demonstrated was his way of saying, "I'm in charge here. I have power and I want you to know it."

Bill was difficult to control when we held physical activities or athletic games. His desire to be king of the mountain led him to outrageous behavior in football, basketball, and swimming. He would push, shove, tackle, and nearly drown the others—anything it took to establish and maintain his superiority. As you can imagine, we were all relieved when Bill entered high school and took his place on the bottom of the totem pole. And I think Bill was, too. In high school he wasn't king of the hill, so he didn't have to constantly assert himself.

Marketing

According to Marcel Danesi, a University of Toronto semiotics professor, teens weren't identified as a cultural group until the 1950s when their image was constructed and solidified in books, magazines, television programs, and movies (think

James Dean).[26] From the fifties forward, the teen industry has kept that image alive, and now a verifiable new group has emerged—tweens.

The push to influence tweens is rooted in demographics. The bulk of baby boomers' offspring is now in the nine-to-fourteen age range, and another surge will be coming along in the next few years. Marketers are bracing for the onslaught.

"It isn't enough just to advertise on television," one ad executive told *The Washington Times.* "You've got to reach the kids throughout their day—in school, as they're shopping at the mall … or at the movies. You've got to become part of the fabric of their lives."[27]

Diane Nye, vice president of marketing for Limited Too, agrees that tweens are the latest hot market. "This is a transition girl," she says, speaking of her store's clientele. "I like to say that she's caught between Barbie and her driver's license."[28]

Canadian cable network YTV, geared expressly toward tweens, surveyed 770 randomly selected tweens in Canada. The YTV report found that Canada's tweens represent almost $1.4 *billion* worth of spending power.[29] How do kids get this kind of money? They receive allowances, as well as money for birthday and holiday gifts. Other tweens baby-sit and earn money for odd jobs.

The YTV tween survey also reported that tweens influence the purchase of $45 billion worth of goods each year.[30] Parents who work all day tend to buy things for their children out of guilt, and noncustodial divorced parents assuage their guilt by spending on gifts or sending money to their children. In addition, nine out of ten tweens influence the purchase of their own clothes and shoes. Eight out of ten have a say in what games, toys, snack foods, and restaurants the family chooses. And believe it or not, three out of ten influence the purchase of a family car.[31] So, if you're thinking of a tween as some whiny kid in a grocery store, pleading for his mother to buy candy, you need to think again. Today's tweens have real purchasing power. James McNeal, who has studied childhood consumerism for decades, proclaims the United States a "filiarchy," a bountiful kingdom ruled by children.[32]

Measuring Maturity

When I was twelve, I thought thirteen was the ideal age—Oh, to be a teenager! When I reached fourteen, I yearned for sixteen so I could drive. When sixteen arrived, the age of high school graduation seemed the perfect one. And when I reached eighteen, twenty-one seemed like the age of the True Adult. Thirty felt like maturity had arrived at last, and forty felt a little odd—sort of like my body was aging faster than my brain. You, too?

Tweens have that same desire for maturity. They have a tendency to swear and smoke and sneak into R-rated movies because these are "adult" privileges they can assume without too much difficulty. Unlike adults, who measure maturity by responsibility, tweens measure maturity by *privileges*.

The tremendous drive for independence that begins during the tweenage years is really the desire for the status of adulthood, with all the privileges tweens covet: the freedom to drive (controlling one's physical surroundings), the freedom from school (controlling one's mental surroundings), and the freedom to choose their own friends and circumstances (controlling one's social surroundings).

When your tweens are tempted to seek adulthood through unwise behaviors, teach them that maturity is not a matter of being able to do as you please, but doing what pleases God, even against overwhelming odds. Teach your children that maturity is not minding a list of do's and don'ts, but following the principles behind the laws in God's Word. True freedom is not the freedom to do wrong, but the ability to do right.

Freedom does not automatically arrive at age eighteen, any more than maturity arrives at twenty-one. True freedom and maturity arrive when a young person develops character that will withstand the tests of this world.

The Media Generation

According to a Kaiser Family Foundation survey of more than three thousand children ages two through eighteen, our children's bedrooms are fully equipped media centers. The Kaiser Family Foundation study found that 65 percent of children ages eight to eighteen have televisions in their bedrooms, and 70 percent have radios. The authors of the Kaiser study wrote that while one generation of Americans experienced a childhood in which "they shared a single black-and-white, three-channel TV with their parents, the next is growing up with a Walkman glued to their ears, one hundred channels in the bedroom, and a World Wide Web of information at their fingertips…. One generation may have flinched at gunshots in a Western; the next generation plays video games with violence so vivid it leaves them ducking to avoid being splattered."[33]

The Kaiser study indicates that on average children spend five hours and twenty-nine minutes every day, seven days a week, with media. For kids eight and older, the average is six hours and forty-three minutes per day—the equivalent of an adult workweek.[34]

"Most parents will be dumbfounded by this," said Donald F. Roberts, a professor of communications at Stanford University. "Most parents will say, 'Not my child.' And most parents will be wrong."[35]

The Canadian children's network, YTV, is targeted directly at tweens. *Canadian Business* reports, "With its bold advertising, cartoon-filled schedule, gory ghost stories, video-game programs, and unapologetic attitude, YTV has emerged as a kind of anti-Sesame Street for today's kids. YTV's slogan is 'You Rule.' Its underlying message: 'We're not even pretending to be good for you.'"[36]

Our kids spend hours watching these types of television programs with little parental supervision and almost no rules. According to diaries kept by children in the Kaiser study, 95 percent of the time older children are watching television their parents are not in the room. Forty-nine percent said there are no household rules about watching TV.

Have you watched television with your children lately? Did you know that Jamie Kellner, CEO of the WB network, said the responsibility of television programmers is to "put on the real world and show the consequences, show the options"? WB's target audience is twelve to thirty-four-year-olds, and its programs frequently feature sexual situations involving teens and young adults.[37]

I have to ask—how can someone in Hollywood understand the real world of *my* teenager? How often do those televised teen sexual encounters result in pregnancy? Do they show characters grappling with post-abortion stress or venereal disease? How often do those cute guys dump the pretty heroines after they've managed to get them into bed for a night of sexual misadventure?

Hmmm?

A survey of 104 top TV creators and executives conducted by the Center for Media and Public Affairs found that the views of the TV "elite" are considerably more liberal than those of most Americans. Ninety-seven percent of the respondents held pro-abortion views, for example, while 86 percent supported the right of homosexuals to teach in public schools, and 51 percent did not regard adultery as wrong.

"People in Hollywood are overwhelmingly left of center," says Robert Lichter, co-director of the Center. "So, you get material on environmentalism, feminism, gay rights. You won't see old-fashioned patriotism, stories on religion, support for the military."[38]

Why is this alarming? First, a recent article in *The Washington Post* proclaimed that the media—television, radio, and computers—may influence your child's development more than you will. "We've always looked at church, school, and home as the primary influences in raising children," said Texas researcher Ellen Wartella. "Now we have to add media to that mix."[39]

Second, the authors of the survey created a "contentedness index" to measure how satisfied children are with their lives. The results showed that the *highest* media users scored *lowest* on the "contentedness index." The authors wrote, "Indicators of discontent such as not getting along with parents, unhappiness at school, and getting into trouble a lot, are strongly associated with high media use."[40]

A third cause for alarm is that most television producers are not producing work designed to educate, inspire, or edify your children. They want to sell products, period. Stanford's Professor Roberts said that even the youngest children are "not an audience, they're a market."[41] And what the media is marketing to our children is "cool."

Danesi says, "They market this cool very nicely of course. Kids think 'I want to be like that. They look like they're having fun.' But it's happening much earlier now. I've seen kids as young as five and six starting to talk and act like teenagers. Rather than playing with Barbie dolls, they're dancing to music videos."[42]

What's a parent to do? You have several options, ranging from tossing out the television to doing nothing at all. I would suggest that you not toss out the television. Instead, limit the amount of time your children spend watching it. Encourage other activities—sports, hobbies, even (dare I say it?) books!

Second, try watching television *with* your children sometime. If you're reading a book, for instance, instead of retreating to your bedroom, sit in the room where your tween is watching TV. With your eyes on the book and your ears tuned to the television, you can monitor what is being said. (The Kaiser Family Study, incidentally, reported that today's children have become proficient at "multi-tasking"—watching TV while working on the computer, for instance. You're probably more proficient at multitasking than you realize!)

By monitoring what's being watched and talking with their tweens and teens about situations that arise in television characters' lives, parents can actively support quality, wholesome programs that support Christian family values. If you see a show you like, write a letter to the producer and praise it to the skies. If a character on a show makes a quick decision to sleep with her boyfriend, talk to your child about it, and point out all the things the television writers ignored. And, in all fairness, sometimes television characters do The Right Thing. Point out those situations as well.

The media is here to stay, and its influence is a strong one. But unless you abdicate your position of influence, you have far more impact on your tween's life than anything else. We must be vigilant and champion the truth. We are responsible for being the primary influencers of the children God has loaned us. So, let's keep an eye on *anything* that enters our children's lives.

Mental Mayhem

No matter how much they may dislike academics, tweens are learning in new and important ways. While a seven-year-old finds it difficult to deal with hypothetical situations, tweens can more easily grasp situations they have never before considered. But such imaginings can lead to difficult mental conundrums.

For instance, suppose we provided a group of tweens with the following information:

- All three-legged elephants are red.
- Sue is carrying a three-legged elephant.

If we then asked, "What color is Sue's elephant?" a tween could easily deduce the correct answer. A seven-year-old, on the other hand, might be confused because three-legged elephants don't exist and no girl could carry one.

How does this new kind of reasoning create problems? Let's look at another example:

- God loves man.
- God creates little babies.
- Many babies are born disfigured.
- If God loves man, why does he create disfigured people?

Young people who have always held the first two statements as absolutely valid will be forced to examine them again in the light of the third statement and resulting question. When faced with such seemingly contradictory facts, many tweens find that everything they have been taught since birth suddenly seems tentative.

Wise parents have insights to draw upon, but tweens don't have that wealth of knowledge and experience. For instance, we know that God does not create disfigured babies out of spite. We understand that we live in a fallen world, and many troubles of the world are a direct or indirect result of sin. Sometimes we have to admit to our children that there are questions and puzzles beyond human understanding or reasoning.

Look at this one:

- Everyone in a family loves everyone else.
- My parents always know what is best for me.
- My parents are getting a divorce.

When faced with this situation, tweens who grew up believing the first two statements will decide that neither can be true in the light of the third. If parents can stop loving each other, then it stands to reason that they don't always have my best interest at heart, and perhaps their next decision for me will be wrong.

You'll see this search for logic in tweens' arguments. "Why can't I date at fourteen?" a girl may ask her parents. "All my friends are dating. I'm responsible and you always tell me I am mature for my age. Don't you trust me?"

Or a boy will say, "I'm the only guy at school who hasn't seen that movie. So what if it's rated R? That doesn't mean anything. The people at the theater don't care, and I hear worse language at school every day. I see that much violence on the news."

Such mental examinations are natural, but too often flustered parents respond to a child's reasoning with, "You can't do that because I said so!" Such authoritarian responses don't work— they only reinforce the child's doubts and ignore his budding logic. Instead of resorting to parental authority, take the time to calmly spell out *your* logical reasons. Your child may not be thrilled with your decision, but at least he'll begin to understand that there are other things to consider when making decisions. And that's really what we need to do—train our children in the decision-making process.

Middle School at a Glance

Sixth-graders and eighth-graders are as different as mustard and custard. In a room filled with swarms of middle school students, anyone with a little experience can easily pick out the sixth-graders. The boys are louder, more compact, and more energetic than their eighth-grade counterparts. Their voices are shriller. They are more outspoken, quicker to smile, quicker to obey, and quicker to sing and participate.

Sixth-grade girls are easy to spot, too. Many of them are still dressed in frills and ribbons. They may still carry a roll of baby fat around their waistlines, and they usually have a shy demeanor. Many of them still have a baby doll propped on their beds at home, and will privately play with the toys of childhood.

Sixth-graders are taking their first steps into the world of middle school students, and many of them are worried sick about it. Stomach pains and headaches on the first day of school are not unusual. They can be worried about forgetting their schedule or not being able to unlock their lockers.

Seventh-graders are another category altogether. They have a year's experience in middle school to their credit, and they strut into our Sunday school room like rowdy peacocks. The girls greet each other with loud squeals of approval, exclaim over each other's outfits, and reserve long rows of chairs for their friends. The peer group is well defined, with members calling or e-mailing each other several times a day.

The boys are still active, but not quite as obvious in their movements. Many of them are becoming accustomed to their new baritone voices, others are adjusting to sudden growth spurts that result in long arms and gangly legs. They make paper airplanes out of handouts and fling spitballs when the adults aren't looking.

Eighth-graders: What a transformation occurs between the seventh and eighth grades. Sudden sophistication! Overnight cool! Somehow, almost magically over the summer, the eighth grade girls seem to grow within an inch of their adult height. They develop full figures. They visit the Clinique counter and begin to wear more makeup than the average working woman. Their hair is blow-dried to near-frizziness, and their attention turns away from the boys of their own age in favor of high school boys.

Eighth-grade boys are growing tall (finally!), developing shoulders, and working out the hitches in their newly deepened voices. Many of them begin to seriously consider asking a girl to "go out" with them during this year. Like the girls, they are curious about sexual matters, and susceptible to influence from older teenagers.

Eighth-graders are far more self-assured than any other tweens. They know they are at the top of the pecking order, and many of them will begin to exercise true leadership potential.

Each level of middle school development holds its own pleasures and challenges. Enjoy them all!

Modesty

My sixth-grade son came home from church after his first Sunday in the middle school department. "How was it?" I asked.

"Fine," he said. "It was neat. I like the youth pastor and they do really cool stuff."

"That's good."

"Yeah, they really do neat things, but...."

I kept quiet, waiting for him to continue, but he didn't.

"What, Son?" I finally asked.

"Well, it's the girls."

"Girls?"

"Yeah. I can't believe what they wear."

I groaned inwardly, knowing exactly what he meant. He's a boy. God designed males to be attracted by sight, and it's hard to maintain custody of your eyes when females wear short skirts and tight sweaters....

Tilly Stephens, an elementary school teacher for twenty-five years, says kids' clothes today are more sophisticated than ever before. "The brevity of the clothes is amazing—preadolescent belly buttons popping out of them. It's sad to look at an eleven-year-old cleavage that's better than you'll ever have," she told a reporter for *The Toronto Star*. "A lot of these girls have very fashion-conscious mothers who enjoy dressing them this way. I don't think at heart the kids are really that much different now. But their mothers let them dress this way. The shoes with the huge platforms, the tighter clothes. And you never saw children wearing black before."[43]

Nancy Dennis, founder of Chickaboom stores for tween girls, says that children today are "growing up faster and nobody can stop it." Her stores sell designer clothing, including slinky tops, slip dresses, and marabou-trimmed sweaters. Chickaboom stores also offer nail polish bars where girls can apply black and glitter nail polish or opt for hair mascara, temporary butterfly tattoos, and glitter gel. "The clothing is not precious and puffy—these kids want to look like teenagers," says Dennis. "They want what's cool, but this is not about making them look twenty-one."[44]

Moms, your tween may refuse to wear ruffles and lace, but don't give up and let her wear the suggestive fashions so popular today. It's important that we teach the importance of modesty. Girls need to be aware that short skirts, tight clothing, and low-cut or barely-there tops send a signal. Any girl who intends to remain chaste and honor the Lord with her body doesn't need to wear sexy lingerie and perfumes called "Follow Me Boy."

Psychologist Rona Novik says wise parents will set limits. "There's a whole generation of parents that equates giving your child independence with giving in to your child," she told a writer for *Newsday*. "You can raise perfectly independent children and still say, 'You can't go to Grandma's house with a skirt that short.'"[45]

"We're living in a day and age," Novik continues, "when young girls are getting the message that they can do everything they put their minds to." On the other hand, she warns, "For a ten- or eleven-year-old, their bodies may develop before their minds click in and they don't understand their own sexuality. When they're out in the world eliciting a sexual response, they may not know how to protect themselves." But, Novik insists, "The most alarming thing of all is parents' difficulty or total failure at setting limits appropriately."

Don't be afraid to say "No" to a certain style. You won't be alone. If you and your daughter are arguing over fashion, give in on the embroidered jeans. Say no to the halter top.

I've already mentioned that each year the ladies of our middle school lay staff stage an "immodest fashion show" for our girls. Dressing to exaggerate, we feature characters such as Laurie Long Legs, Teddie Too Tight, and Bertha Bosom. While the girls giggle and cheer for our overly underdressed ladies, we try to point out that immodesty is a very real problem.

We held our annual show last month. After the models left the platform I turned to the girls and tried to sum up the lesson of the evening. "Everyone knows that men and women are created differently," I told the seventy middle school girls present. "And you need to understand this—you may see a good-looking guy without his shirt and think, 'Wow!', but when a guy sees a girl who is immodestly dressed, he has an entirely different reaction."

One rather precocious seventh-grader lifted a brow. "How do you know?" she challenged. "I don't think it's any different at all."

Caught off guard, I stared at her for a long moment. I didn't feel it was the time or place to go into a lesson on human physiology and explain exactly *how* we know men are physically stimulated by sight, and I'll admit that I was a little rattled by her confident attitude. By her comment and body language, she seemed to be saying that she knew *all* about boys, and her experience had proven I was dead wrong....

"I'm a married woman, honey," I finally told her. "Trust me—men are different. If you don't believe me, maybe you should ask your mother."

Moms, please be aware that immodesty is no kindness to the men and boys in your daughter's life. It's teasing, pure and simple. Teasing is cruel, unfair, and just plain wrong. It is offering something that cannot righteously be offered ... or accepted.

The lesson of modesty is not only for girls—it has an application for boys, too. Young men need to know that it's human to see, but it's wrong to *look*.

Our Florida town has the dubious distinction of being home to several hot dog vendors who park their carts along the highway in the midst of rush hour. There's nothing wrong with selling hot dogs, of course, but when the seller is young, female, and wearing nothing but a bikini top and a thong, well—it's a wonder we haven't had more traffic accidents. My pastor always says it's not a sin to drive by and *see* the hot dog vendors, but you're asking for trouble if you make a U-turn to go back for a second *look!*

Moms and dads, talk to your sons and daughters about modesty. Dads, you can be the deciding vote on what your daughter wears—sometimes a male perspective can be invaluable. Moms, demonstrate through your own clothing that a woman doesn't have to be immodest to be fashionable and well dressed.

Normal Tweenage Problems

In his book *Relief for Hurting Parents*, Buddy Scott lists the following ordinary problems of adolescence and cautions parents not to bring out the big guns of discipline for these fairly predictable behaviors:

- Putting off chores
- Doing chores just good enough to get by
- Forgetting to weed-whack one side of the house
- Putting off homework
- Not wanting to go to bed
- Spending too much time watching TV
- Staying too long on the phone or the computer
- Hating to get out of bed
- Forgetting to brush teeth
- Losing the retainer
- Making an occasional bad grade
- Having occasional trouble with teachers
- Leaving candy and gum wrappers in your car
- Hating things loved yesterday
- Spending money carelessly
- Holding the refrigerator door open while deciding what to eat
- Being unsatisfied with what parents are providing
- Teasing brothers and sisters
- Demanding more independence by relating how good other kids have it
- Resisting going to church at times
- Forgetting to thank people for gifts

The following are more serious problems that deserve Heavy Duty Parental Attention:

- Staying out past curfew
- Running away from home
- Skipping school
- Failing classes
- Taking or selling drugs
- Drinking underage
- Running with a bad crowd
- Shoplifting
- Exhibiting an ugly attitude[46]

When you're about to lose your temper and ground your child for life, make certain the offense isn't a normal tweenage problem. Tomorrow, you'll be glad you backed off.

Now it came to pass...

My Mary Engelbreit page-a-day-calendar for *today* featured a photograph of a woman embracing two robotic-looking creatures in baggy pants. Mary had labeled the woman as (A) The Mother, and the creatures as (B) Alien Teenagers. Beneath the drawing was a single phrase: "This too shall pass."

The Scriptures echo the thought:

- Joshua 10:1, "Now it came to pass, when Adoni-zedec king of Jerusalem had heard ..."
- Ruth 1:1, "Now it came to pass in the days when the judges ruled ..."
- 1 Samuel 14:1, "Now it came to pass upon a day, that Jonathan the son of Saul ..."
- 2 Samuel 1:1, "Now it came to pass after the death of Saul ..."
- 2 Kings 18:1, "Now it came to pass in the third year of Hoshea ..."

- 1 Chronicles 17:1, "Now it came to pass, as David sat in his house ..."

Do you see a pattern here? Things come ... to pass. Over and over again, *twenty-four times* in the King James Version, the Lord assures us that situations come to pass! And if you think I'm interpreting Scripture loosely, listen to what else the Bible tells us about trials:

These trials are only to test your faith, to show that it is strong and pure. It is being tested as fire tests and purifies gold—and your faith is far more precious to God than mere gold. So if your faith remains strong after being tried by fiery trials, it will bring you much praise and glory and honor on the day when Jesus Christ is revealed to the whole world.

1 PETER 1:7

Dear friends, don't be surprised at the fiery trials you are going through, as if something strange were happening to you.

1 PETER 4:12

Give all your worries and cares to God, for he cares about what happens to you.

1 PETER 5:7

When trials and heartbreaks come, moms and dads, they come to pass. The cloud that won't allow even a single ray of sunshine into your house today will dissipate tomorrow. The child who is keeping you awake tonight will settle down next week. There may be other nights when you walk the floor, but this present trial will come to pass.

Hang in there, moms and dads. A million other parents have felt what you're feeling. And those of us who are believers can attest to the fact that God is faithful. We love our children, but he loves them more.

Thank God, the hard times come to pass.

Other Adults

"Disciplining my kid is easy," a mother told me not long ago. "All I have to do is suggest that I take him to meet with your husband. He thinks so much of Gary that he shapes up right away."

We exchanged a laugh over that one, but there's an important truth in her statement—middle school students are at the age when they seek out other significant adults to admire, trust, and befriend. Many times they will go to one of these other adults for counsel and advice. While this may hurt your feelings, it's natural and normal. And if you've been wise, you've placed your children in a position where the significant other adults in his life will tell them exactly what *you* would have told them, had they gone to you.

As the invisible umbilical cord between parents and children stretches and thins, tweens begin to form other relationships. They establish their places in a peer group, reach out for new adult influences, and begin to open themselves to a host of friendships. Many parents are jealous of the affection their children lavish on new adult friends such as youth workers, teachers, or neighbors. Parents often feel overlooked and underappreciated—and frankly, they probably are. But it's okay. In a few more years, you'll be the one they're calling for money.

Parental Protection

A story to share with your older tweens …

Corey and Jenny were riding home in Corey's car from their date. Jenny was a little surprised when Corey stopped on a deserted road.

"So, Jenny," he said as the car engine died. "I really like you."

She gave him a shy smile. "I really like you, too."

Corey's grin broadened. "That's good. Because when two people like each other a lot, they should try to deepen their relationship. They want to share everything."

Jenny giggled. "I talk to you on the phone for an hour every night. And we've been going together six weeks. This is the deepest relationship I've ever had."

"That's good." Corey rested his arm on her bucket seat. "So, uh—do you want to hop in the back?"

Jenny's eyes widened. "Of course not! I'd rather stay up here with you!"

Corey bit his lip and looked out the window. Things weren't going the way he had planned. Either Jenny had just developed a case of terminal blondeness, or she was just teasing.

"I don't think you know what I mean," he said, placing his hand on her silky hair. "I really want to give myself to you. I want to show you how much I love you, and that means—well, that means having sex."

Jenny remained silent, and after a moment Corey risked a glance at her face. She was staring at her hands in her lap, but after a minute she looked up and gave him a confident smile. "I understand. But we need protection. Can you drive me to the drug store we passed a few minutes ago?"

"Sure." Unable to believe his luck, Corey cranked the car and slammed it into gear.

"And I'll need a quarter once we get there."

Corey pulled out onto the road, then gave Jenny a puzzled look. "A quarter?"

She nodded. "Yeah. My dad said if this ever came up, I should just get to the nearest phone and call him. He said he'd be all the protection I'd ever need."

Our middle school drama teams used to perform that little story. It's a cute, effective way to stress several points—first, kids do pressure each other sexually, and second, that parents should be an important part of their children's dating lives.

Parents

When our son was about twelve, I realized how little he knew about us, his parents, when he was talking about college. He said something about wanting to get a college degree since his dad didn't have one.

"What do you mean?" I asked. "Your dad went to college."

"I know, but he never finished," my son answered. "He did-n't get a degree."

I was stunned. "Your father has two degrees—one in psychology, and one in engineering."

My son couldn't believe it; the shock was evident on his face. For most of his life, for some obscure reason he had believed that his father had dropped out of college. I have no idea where he got that idea, but that was part of the image he had of his father. Learning the truth forced him to readjust all his thinking.

Although it often seems our kids would like us to evaporate, most tweens still love and appreciate their parents. While commenting upon the media's influence on tweens, syndicated columnist Maggie Gallagher made a telling observation: "The price children pay [for growing up too quickly] was suggested most poignantly by the president of the Cartoon Network, who, when asking kids to suggest contest prizes, was amazed at the number who spoke not of an all-expense-paid trip to Disneyland, but of spending a 'whole day with my mom or dad.'" In addition, noted Gallagher, "Kids ... are now telling marketers they don't like to see cartoons in which their fragile, elusive, uncertain parents are mocked."[47]

Parents are still important. The authors of *The Roller-Coaster Years* point out that once their children hit the tween years many parents assume the following:

- Young children need parents more than older children do.
- Young adolescents need to be left alone in order to become independent.
- My child has a personal life now and it doesn't include me.
- Ten- to fifteen-year-olds care more about what their peers think than what their parents think.[48]

All of the above statements are *false!* Your kids need you as much if not more now than in the past. Tweens want to step out and try new things on their own, but they'll come hustling back when they run into trouble. Be sure to be available.

Parties and Hospitality

How do you throw a great party for middle school students? Put away anything breakable. Order lots of pizza, provide soda and napkins, and give them room to roam—outdoors, if possible. It's that simple.

Don't waste a lot of time worrying about atmosphere or decorations, just give them room to work out their energy and food to replenish it.

Because I'm a youth pastor's wife, many times people will say things like, "Oh, I suppose you have youth activities at your house all the time."

Are you *crazy*?

We tried it for a while. When we were first married, I thought part of the job was having weekly Bible studies at the house. In the first week, my olive-green carpet was permanently stained with red Virginia clay, so later we carpeted the den in orange commercial carpeting. It wasn't pretty, but that didn't matter. We bought den furniture that was little more than two-by-fours with cushions, and fashioned a game room in the basement. Tweens break things, so we tried to make the room as indestructible as possible.

Then my husband's ministry grew, and I accepted a couple of hard facts. First, there's no scriptural command that says I have to throw open every door and bedroom to hordes of tramping tweens. I am given to hospitality, but not on demand, and not with one hundred kids at a time.

Second, once we had children, I came to realize that my family needs a place to call our own. We have nicknamed our house "Hunt Haven," and that's what my home is—a haven away from work, away from school, away from the rest of the world. I want my kids to be able to come home and not feel that they have to share every aspect of their lives with everyone else. We have guests in occasionally. When we do, my kids tend to retreat and adopt an unusual self-conscious attitude. They aren't comfortable in their own home when strangers are about, and I don't want them to feel this way for extended periods of time.

Lest you think I've become a total Grinch, I'm happy to host lay staff meetings, the annual eighth-grade party (we hold it outdoors), and other special events. I actually enjoy being a hostess and throwing parties for tweens. But experience has taught me that being gracious doesn't mean being a doormat.

So—tween parties can be fun, but batten down the hatches and keep the crowd to a manageable number!

Peer Pressure

Years ago I saw a group of young people perform a variation of the following fable as a skit. It's another good story to tell your children—at any age.

Once upon a time there lived a farmer, his wife, and their donkey, a sweet animal they called Hiney. The farmer and his wife loved Hiney very much.

But times were hard on the farm, and the farmer and his wife knew the time had come to sell Hiney. So they put a rope around his neck and led him toward town.

They hadn't gone very far, though, when a group of old men came by. "Look at those silly people," they said. "One of them could be riding that donkey!"

The old man didn't want to be thought of as silly, so he climbed up on Hiney and let his wife lead the donkey toward town.

They hadn't gone very far when a group of old women came by. "Look at that awful man!" they said. "Riding that donkey while his wife walks!"

Well, the old man didn't want to be thought of as awful, so he made his wife climb on the donkey, too.

They hadn't gone very far when a group of teenagers came by. "Look at those cruel people," the teens said. "Both of those big people on that little donkey!"

The old man didn't want to be thought of as cruel, so he and his wife climbed off the donkey. What could he do? He couldn't ride, he couldn't walk … so he and his wife decided to carry the donkey.

Carrying a donkey is not an easy thing, especially if the donkey doesn't want to be carried. As misfortune would have it, as they were crossing a wooden bridge, the farmer and his wife dropped poor Hiney. He fell into the river and swam away.

The moral of the story is: don't give in to peer pressure, or you'll lose your Hiney every time.

Urie Bronfenbrenner, an authority on child development from Cornell University, has noted that the adolescent peer group has the potential for becoming a destructive force. "At least in the United States," he wrote, "the peer group tends to undermine adult socialization efforts and to encourage egocentrism, aggression, and antisocial behavior." He also said that a survey of American sixth-graders found that "those children who were the most peer-oriented were those who reported engaging most often in antisocial activities such as lying to adults, smoking, and using bad language."[49]

Not only can peer groups promote undesirable behavior, they are also often responsible for repressing individual tastes, values, and emotions. Many would-be musicians give up music during adolescence because time spent practicing is not as important as time spent with friends. Girls whose one beauty is their hair will cut it, perm it, and color it if their friends are doing the same.

Clothes are the uniform of the peer group. Just last week I looked at a long row of tweens and noticed that they were wearing different variations of the same style skirt, the same style shoe, the same style sweater. They looked like a row of matching salt and pepper shakers!

Peer pressure is usually knocked as something bad, but it can be a great positive force, too. Gary and I have used the peer dynamic to get tweens to encourage their friends to attend church, to establish the habit of daily prayer and Bible reading, and to be examples to their friends. Friends can influence each other for good or bad, but there's no denying the power of peer pressure.

How can you make certain your child is not being unduly affected by his peers? The key lies in balance. Until the tween years, adults were the primary influencers of your child's life. Now the pendulum is swinging toward peers, but don't abdicate your position. Some breaking away from parental guidance and authority is natural and normal, but studies have shown that the peer-oriented child is more a product of parental disregard than of the attractiveness of the peer group. John Janeway Conger writes that a child will turn "to his age mates less by choice than by default. The vacuum left by the withdrawal of parents and adults from the lives of children is filled with an undesired—and possibly undesirable—substitute of an age-segregated peer group."[50]

Quite simply, parents who spend time with their tweens will continue to be the primary influence in their children's lives. When the relationship between parents and children is strong, parental influence will overshadow peer influence. However, parents who let their children withdraw from the family circle will allow the peer relationship to become the most important influence in a child's head and heart. In 1981, Daniel Yankelovich did a study called "New Rules." Former U.S. Secretary of Education William Bennett, author of *The Book of Virtues,* remarked on the Yankelovich study:

[Yankelovich] found evidence of something that should distress all of us concerned about young people. He suggests in his study that parents began to put the raising of children at a lower priority in their lives. He describes what we might call a terrible compact, a deal. As he says in his report, "We shall demand less from you, children, and in return we'll make less sacrifice for you." Yankelovich talks about the statistically demonstrable fact that many couples were less willing to stay together for the sake of their children during this period of 1960 to 1980. Yankelovich talks about an increasing tendency for parents to say they wish to live their own lives, even if it means less time with their children."[51]

I don't need to see the statistics to know the above statements are true. Every week I talk to tweens who are tossed back and forth like the wind, shuttled from one parent to another like excess baggage. Is it any wonder that so many kids turn to their peers for a sense of belonging and stability?

Moms and dads, take time to be with your child. I know it's not easy when both parents are working and daily demands are high, but make a point of asking your child to do something with you. My daughter and I have taken short trips together; sometimes I'll do something as simple as take her to a movie. My husband has discovered that he enjoys prime time with the kids in the car. When they're too young to drive, they need chauffeuring, and that is a wonderful time to talk. So turn off the radio, clear your mind, and have a heart-to-heart with your kids in the car.

Privacy versus Snooping
A few years ago, one of my former middle schoolers stopped me at church. Rochelle had matured into a lovely young lady, and

seemed to be enjoying high school. "Angie," she asked, "you wouldn't snoop through your daughter's bedroom, would you?"

I thought a moment. "Yes and no," I told her. "No, as long as I don't have any reason to suspect anything unusual. But yes—if I thought for one instant that she was in trouble, I wouldn't hesitate to look around. The virtuous woman in Proverbs 31 'looks well to the ways of her household,' and I believe she knew what was happening in the lives of her children."

I could tell from the look on Rochelle's face that my answer surprised her. She walked away without saying much, but the other day she called me from another state, where she is now a youth pastor's wife and pregnant with her first child. While I listened and murmured "uh huh," a lot, Rochelle proceeded to tell me about a girl in their youth group who was sneaking out of the house to see a boy her parents had declared off-limits. "I hope I told them the right thing," Rochelle said, "but I told them to check her diary, to look for notes in her room, to do everything they could think of to know what was going on in her life. This guy is bad news, he's been in trouble with the law, and he uses drugs. So I told them to do anything they could to protect her."

I smiled into the phone. "Rochelle, do you remember asking me if I'd ever snoop in my daughter's room?"

"Yes, I do," she answered, "and I remember being shocked when you said you would. But now it all makes sense. You stop stubborn two-year-olds from harming themselves, and sometimes you've got to stop stubborn sixteen-year-olds from doing the same thing."

My daughter spends hours behind a closed and locked bedroom door. Many times I've stood in the hall and wondered what she's doing in there, but I don't worry too much. I know she may be reading, dreaming, writing, trying out a new hair-do, or just staring into the mirror.

There are so-called child experts who will tell you that snooping is wrong and unethical. I disagree. If I thought my child was involved in premarital sex, using drugs, dating a criminal, or engaging in some other risky behavior, I would certainly want to know. I can't help her, I can't even pray specifically, unless I know what's happening in her life.

As I write this, the world is still reeling in horror over the massacre at Columbine High School, and fingers of blame are pointing at the parents of the two boys who killed their class-mates and then themselves. I don't know what went on in those families, but I'm reasonably sure those parents had no idea what their sons were planning. Too many parents have given their children too much privacy.

Privacy is something children need and deserve—to a point—but it is not a God-ordained right. Look well to the ways of your children.

Quick Comebacks for Come-on Lines

It may not be this year or next, but when your kids begin to think about dating, it's time to drill the following lines into your children's heads. Connie Marshner has given us snappy, practical answers for the typical lines guys and girls use on each other.

When one says: "You don't know how to have any fun."
The other can reply: "Yes, I do. I've had a great time. Let's just leave it at that, okay?"

When he says: "You don't understand. Guys have to have sex."
She says: "That's silly. Nobody ever died of abstinence before, and you won't be the first."

When she says: "I love you so much that I want to give you something more."
He can say: "Okay, so give me your self-control, and let me keep what I cherish, control over my own body."

When one says: "Don't you love me?"
The other can answer: "Well, frankly, if you're that kind of person, no."

When someone says: "Everybody does it, you know."
The answer is: "I'm not everybody."

If someone says: "I'll bet you're just scared."
The comeback is: "Of venereal disease, yes. Of illegitimate pregnancy, you bet."

If he says: "But I'll take care of you."
She can answer: "Thanks, but I can take care of myself for now."

If one says: "It's only natural."
The other responds: "So is death, but I don't want to practice that, either."[52]

Got it? These are so good, they're worth memorizing!

Small Rebellions

Although a certain degree of rebellion is natural and to be expected, many parents are caught off guard by the constant battle of wills with their tweens. The child who has always been trustworthy may suddenly begin to lie to his parents so he can go along with the peer group he now reveres as his guiding authority. Kids who used to help around the house will now forget to clean their rooms, return their dishes, and feed the dog. You think it's rebellion; it's more likely to be simple childish forgetfulness.

For the little rebellions that arise when your tween tests your rules (curfew breaking, not calling as promised, ignoring or postponing a parental request), it's important that you reinforce your rules. First, though, explain *why* you hold these standards. Don't patronize or antagonize your child by resorting to that old parental favorite, "You'll do this because I said so!"

Remember that your tween is developing new mental processes; he's learning to think for himself. So explain the principles behind your rules, and make sure your principles are valid. You want Nicole home by nine on school nights so she can get her homework done and get a good night's sleep. You want Jaysen to call and check in because you love him and worry about him when you don't know where he is. You don't want Holly to hang out with Natalie because Natalie's older brother has been known to offer drugs to younger kids. Give your reasons, even if your kids squawk about them.

When it comes time to discipline your tween for small rebellions, safeguard his trust and be sure that the discipline is appropriate for the infraction. Make the circle of confession as large as the circle of transgression and no larger. Don't make the broken rule and subsequent discipline a matter of public record and family history.

Parental love should be like God's—once a small rebellion is forgiven, bury it in the sea of forgetfulness.

Large-Scale Rebellion

Why do tweens and teens rebel? Aside from the small rebellions that result primarily from testing parental standards, rebellion on a grander scale often results from a broken promise. A study by Arthur L. Stinchcombe showed that adolescents believe in the law of cause and effect—in other words, certain behaviors should earn certain results.[53] Good performance in school, for instance, should result in good grades; good grades should result in parental approval. When the expected chain of results is broken and the unspoken promise is not kept (a good performance in school merits only a C from a tough teacher, or the good grades are greeted with parental nonchalance), the adolescent rebels against the system and refuses to try again. *If the system doesn't work*, he reasons, *why should I try?*

The broken promise can arise in any area—family, school, even spiritual life. Many times I've heard the following from rebellious tweens whose parents have just divorced: "I tried to be good and make it easier for Mom and Dad, but they split up anyway." Other tweens may be angry with God for the death of a parent: in their eyes, God promised to protect the family, but then he took a parent away.

An adolescent who experiences this rebellion against God, his family, or the system sees no use in preparing for any sort of future. All he has been brought up to believe has failed. He can see no purpose in self-restraint, good performance, faith, or prayer. All that matters, he reasons, is finding pleasure and happiness for the moment.

How do you help a child suffering from this loss of hope?

Communication is the key. If your child will not open up to you, engage the help of another adult you trust and he likes: an uncle, a teacher, a professional counselor. Let them talk alone, and ask your adult ally to find out what has disappointed your child. Once the problem is identified, you will know whether your child needs to learn how to handle anger, hurt, or disappointment. Bad things do come into our lives, but these things are not meant to break us. God allows trials in order to make us stronger, to develop the qualities of perseverance and courage.

When your child is able and willing to talk to you, be sure to convey the following messages:

- You've noticed changes in him that have perplexed you. Apologize if you have responded incorrectly or ignored the problem in the past.
- Adolescence is a period of change, and frustration is a necessary part of the tween/teenage years. Although he is facing pressures that result from being caught between the worlds of childhood and adulthood, you love him tremendously and will do all you can to guide him through these years.
- He is growing toward maturity and soon he will be on his own. As he grows, his freedom and responsibilities will increase, but on a timetable established by you, his parents. Just because the law says he can drive at sixteen, or just because everyone else is dating at fifteen, doesn't necessarily mean you will grant automatic permission.
- He is not grown yet! As much as he'd like to be able to do as he pleases, he cannot have the freedom of an adult without the corresponding responsibilities. The irresponsibility of childhood and the freedom of adulthood do not go together.

- You are responsible to God for his safety, well-being, and spiritual development. Let your child know that you will try to be more receptive to his feelings and needs, and that you will carefully consider any requests for new privileges, but there will be times when you must say no. When that happens, no amount of whining or pouting will change your decision. As parents, you will strive to be fair and firm.

The apostle James wrote, "Dear brothers and sisters, whenever trouble comes your way, let it be an opportunity for joy. For when your faith is tested, your endurance has a chance to grow. So let it grow, for when your endurance is fully developed, you will be strong in character and ready for anything" (James 1:2-4).

Schedules

Kirsten, my eleven-year-old, started sixth grade today. It was her first time to change classes and actually get a schedule. She picked up the schedule last Thursday at registration, and since that time she has Xeroxed six copies of it, taped one in each of her notebooks, and memorized it. She's terrified of forgetting it and not knowing where to go.

Then she numbered each part of her wardrobe (blue shirt #1, red shirt #2, flared jeans #3), and did a number-coded calendar to determine what to wear each day for a month. Monday is one, three, and six. She numbered her hairstyles, too. Tuesday she'll wear hairstyle number two, which is a ponytail with the butterfly barrette.

The really funny thing is that after she worked for hours on her schedule, she threw it away because it wasn't quite right. I think she really just wanted to spend hours dwelling on that first week of school and work it all out in her mind because she was nervous about it.

Self-Esteem

One of my youth pastors made us memorize this little ditty:

I!
I am!
I am me!
I am me and I am good!
I am me and I am good 'cause God don't make no junk!

Though we chanted it with the hysterical irreverence of youth, that little refrain got me through many a heartache. If the boy I adored didn't like me or if I failed at some goal, that was okay. I wasn't a failure, because God loved me. I wasn't perfect and I wasn't always good, but Jesus Christ lived inside me, and his goodness could shine through me.

Teach your tween that little chant. Tell your son or daughter that the love you feel for him or her goes beyond "I love you because you're my kid." Specify positive attributes that you appreciate in your child. When he does wrong—and he will—don't say, "You're dumb," but, "You did a dumb thing today. And I know you can learn to choose the right things."

One caveat—in this era when it's politically correct to reinforce self-esteem, it's easy to go overboard and impart the wrong message. Have you ever visited a family where the children ruled the two resident adults? It's a sad situation. *Self-esteem does not equal self-centeredness.* We are to know that we are loved by God and created for a purpose, but part of that purpose is to esteem others better than ourselves and live as *servants.* Jesus himself told us that he came to minister to others, and we are to model our lives after him.

The best way to impart self-esteem to your child? One, tell him you love him. Two, teach him to serve. Take him to a nursing home and deliver cards and small gifts when it's *not* a holiday; encourage your child to do a kindness for the neighbor next door. That flush of good feeling is priceless, and I think it's the kind of self-esteem God wants us to enjoy.

Sex Education

While some boys and girls seem to remain innocent and virtually untouched by prevailing attitudes (I know nine-year-olds who unashamedly play with Cabbage Patch dolls), most would prefer to look and dress like the older kids. According to Michael Thompson, co-author of *Raising Cain: Protecting the*

Emotional Life of Boys, by the time they reach the seventh and eighth grade, boys and girls in increasing numbers engage in oral sex, which they don't think of as sex but as just "fooling around" (sound familiar?).[54]

Ready for the statistics?

- Most tweens have not had intercourse. At age fifteen, eight in ten girls and seven in ten boys are virgins.[55]
- Most young people begin having sex in their mid to late teens, about eight years before they marry. More than half of seventeen-year-olds have had intercourse.[56]
- While 93 percent of teenage women report that their first intercourse was voluntary, one-quarter of these young women report that it was unwanted.[57] They were pressured.
- For seven out of ten young women who first had sex before age thirteen, their first sexual experience was either unwanted or nonvoluntary.[58]
- Every year three million teens acquire a sexually transmitted disease.[59] Teens have higher rates of gonorrhea than do sexually active men and women aged twenty to forty-four.[60]
- Each year, almost one million teenage women—10 percent of all women aged fifteen to nineteen—become pregnant.[61] Thirteen percent of all U.S. births are to teens.[62]
- Nearly four in ten teen pregnancies, excluding those ending in miscarriage, are terminated by abortion.[63]

Lots of kids are sexually active these days. We see teenage mothers on the street and we hear the statistics. We are bombarded by sexual messages from music, advertising, and television. It is not surprising that today's permissive attitudes have encouraged premarital sex even among Christian young people.

It is important that moms and dads explain the tremendous physical changes that are about to take place in their tween's body. Someone must do it. Parents who are shy about talking frankly about sex may ask a youth leader to talk privately to their child. At our church, every year we have a Girls Only/Guys Only session to which we invite moms and dads. In this session for sixth-, seventh-, and eighth-graders, we talk openly and honestly about the differences between men and women.

In my class with the girls, I describe what has come to be known as "the Ladder of Passion," detailing the various levels of physical intimacy. Meanwhile, Gary talks openly with the boys about pornography, lust, and masturbation. Tweens will learn about sex sooner or later, and it is better for them to learn from someone who can explain God's plan.

We invite parents to this meeting for two reasons: first, because we don't want the kids to misrepresent what we say, and second, because we want our discussion to act as a springboard for further discussions at home. If we can help "break the ice" with parents and tweens, we're happy to do it.

Connie Marshner, author of *Decent Exposure: How to Teach Your Children About Sex*, believes Christian kids are literally being sent into a war zone. She says Christian parents must educate and fortify their kids. The challenge is not too great nor is the battle too far gone.

"You can succeed as a parent in today's world," Connie says. "Despite living in a culture with values and expectations that work to draw your child into a sexually promiscuous, self-centered lifestyle, you can win the battle. You can create a Christian atmosphere in your home, discuss the sexual part of life openly and honestly, and instill self-discipline in your child.

You can be the proud parent of a child who honors God in thought, word, and deed."[64]

If Christian parents have a general failing, Connie once told me in a telephone interview, "it is the obliviousness to the threat of the popular culture. It militates against Christian family values every step of the way and most parents don't realize it. They think, 'Oh, that music is harmless'; or 'That movie won't hurt anybody.' But that emphatically is not true. There is a lot of harm. Parents don't realize that a systematic attack is being waged by the world at large against our young people and against Christian values."

Some kids, however, are winning the battle. What do we know about young people who are not sexually active? According to AANCHOR (An Alternative National Curriculum on Responsibility), these kids tend to live with two parents who are interested in them, they have at least a C average in school, they have plans for their futures, they don't date at an early age, their parents have moderately strict discipline and a moderately large number of rules about dating, and they tend to be churchgoers and take their religion seriously.

Marshner believes parents should not teach sex education as much as self-education. "It's *self*-control they need, not sex control," she told me. "There are three phases of education, and all three go on simultaneously throughout life. The first level is factual information about biology and God's Word and our bodies. This should begin when a child is very young."

Former Surgeon General C. Everett Koop agrees. When I had the opportunity to interview him a few years ago, he told me that children should be told about the basics of biology as soon as they begin to ask questions:

As soon as youngsters begin to talk and ask questions, they have a concern and interest in their own anatomy and where babies come from. When they get to be about six, they lose interest in sex until they are about nine. You don't have to worry much about them between six and nine. But when they are nine, they really begin to develop a curiosity and this is the ideal time to teach children.

Teach them before they themselves become involved in adolescence and are very concerned about their own sexuality. At that point you're not teaching the abstract, but something they are deeply involved with and very embarrassed to talk about.[65]

Your child's questions about sex should be answered truthfully and to the extent that the young person wants to know. "The Talk" should not be a one-time event, but several smaller discussions about physical maturation, physical attraction, dating behavior, and so on. Above all, sex should be presented as a natural and God-given gift intended for marriage.

Sex education has to be taught with accompanying moral guidelines. If it is offered without values, sex education becomes lessons in biology and sexual technique.

Consider this analogy. Suppose you take your eleven-year-old out to the garage and give him a detailed introduction to your car. You show him the engine, you give him a set of keys, you even provide a crash helmet in the back seat (just in case, you tell your child, you decide to take her out for a spin and get into trouble). Then you go into the house and resolve never to mention the subject again, even though you know your kid is continually surrounded with movies and music in which the joys of driving are glorified. You're content to hope he waits until he is legally entitled to drive.

Why should he?

We must give our children more than biological facts. They need our love and support. They need a values system that governs every area of their lives, not just their sexuality. And they need a strong sense of self-esteem and the knowledge that a loving God created them for a particular purpose.

Many parents hesitate to bring up the discussion of sex because they're embarrassed or afraid that talking about sex will somehow encourage it. The opposite is usually true: Kids who can talk openly with their parents are more likely to delay sexual involvement.

The second part of sex education is teaching our children how to remain chaste. "We have to instill in the child's heart both a desire to do what is right and the belief that he is capable of doing what is right," says Marshner. "This involves developing a whole series of virtues: obedience, temperance, patience, modesty, self-control, and self-esteem.

"Parents don't often think about the third level of sex education. We have to give our children practical help to empower them to do what is right. They have to have our help in dating and in knowing what to expect from the opposite sex. They need our practical battlefield experience. Nobody tells them that if a guy invites you up to look at his pictures he might have something else in mind. They need to know what to say when kids hang around and talk about their sexual accomplishments. They need to learn ways to say, 'No,' besides just, 'because the Bible says it's wrong.' They need to know the dangers of AIDS and the other sexually transmitted diseases they can get, and they need to be able to articulate their self-respect."[66]

In an age when AIDS runs rampant and teenage pregnancy and abortion destroy the innocence of youth and the promise of the future, we must not forfeit our responsibility to our children. Our schools will not teach about Christian responsibility, God's command for purity, or that self-control is a fruit of the Spirit and available to every Christian.

If we are going to teach our children, we must give them more than the sexual "thou shalt not's." One sixteen-year-old boy sarcastically told *People* magazine, "The only kind of discussion that parents want is one that ends with 'Gee, Mom and Dad, you're so right and I'm not sexually active and won't be at least till I graduate from high school.'"

Christian parents have too often been guilty of simply looking children in the eye and saying, "Premarital sex is a sin. Don't do it!" Now is the time to open our eyes, put away our embarrassment, pull together our courage, and begin saying something more.

Back to the analogy: yes, the car is in the garage. Acknowledge it. But don't give implicit permission by saying, "I know all kids fool around with this kind of thing," and don't walk away from the topic. Sexual issues are a part of your older tween and teen's life, so be available and open when your kids want to talk.

Shopping

If you're one of those people who loves to spend the day at the mall just looking, you're not going to relate to this next story. I'm a list shopper. I make a list, dash to the store where I know the item will be on the shelf, and pick it up. Occasionally, if I have time to spare and a self-indulgent attitude, I will walk through the clearance or sale items, and treat myself to an unexpected and impulsive bargain.

My daughter, on the other hand, is a browser. She loves to go to the mall, and she loves to look. She'll look at every single item on a twenty-foot rack, carefully examining sweaters, jeans, and shirts, then walk away without finding anything that suits her taste. If I'm not in an unhurried and indulgent mood, I've learned not to shop with her. Fortunately, my husband realizes that the long drive to the mall is a great way to spend time with our daughter, so he often volunteers to take her. He probably shops even less than I do, but he's a great bargain hunter in the men's department.

An article in a London newspaper was written by a mother of my mindset. Of shopping with her tween daughter, Phoebe, Jane Lovatt wrote:

> I loathe clothes-shopping with Phoebe and I can see why the feeling is mutual. She still winces at the memory of that terrible Saturday afternoon when I sat on the floor of Gap Kids and shouted, "I want to go!" I always feel like a hen-pecked husband, dragged along to pick up the bills. Even when I take comforting sandwiches to eat in the changing rooms while Phoebe tries on a million and one outfits I still get bored and cross.[67]

The moral of this story is: most tweens and teens require time to shop. After all, their funds are limited, so they must carefully examine their choices and rethink their decisions. So if you're in a hurry, don't shop with a tween.

Smoking

Along with bad language, smoking is one of the activities tweens adopt because it makes them feel more grown-up. Like sneaking a beer, smoking offers an element of danger, the flouting of authority, and the cachet of cool. But smoking often leads to more involved drug use. If a child never starts to smoke cigarettes, the odds are great that he will never try any drugs.

Those who smoke cigarettes find it natural to move up to marijuana; of those who smoke marijuana, nearly 60 percent will go on to try other illicit drugs. If a child never smokes marijuana, the odds are ninety-eight-to-one that he or she will never try any other illegal drug.

Why do kids who do drugs usually start with cigarettes? Because cigarette smoking is an easy way to assert "my body is my own and I will do with it as I please." Kids want to belong to the bold group whose devil-may-care attitude reflects the independence and status tweens admire. Smoking lends an air of toughness to boys and sophistication to girls. Look at the magazine cigarette ads—the ads are either ultra-macho or ultra-chic. Smoking can also be a symbol of absolute rebellion. Adults warn kids about smoking, so when a child is angry and rebellious, he defiantly lights up.

How can we fight smoking among tweens? Let's dispel the cachet of coolness. There's no one better equipped to teach us how to do that than former U.S. Surgeon General C. Everett Koop. A few years ago I interviewed him and asked what parents could do to discourage their children from smoking. His answer:

> You can point out the fact that smoking is not a habit you can pick up and discard when you want to. Nicotine is the most addictive drug in our society. The younger you start, the more difficult it is to quit. We have to point out to kids that there are many disadvantages—your breath stinks, you're not attractive to other people, and if you're an athlete you certainly cut down on your stamina. The health benefits of not smoking are tremendous.[68]

So, moms and dads, though you and I both know the health effects are far more important than halitosis, bad breath is a far more persuasive argument with a tween who considers himself practically immortal. So, do whatever you must—including ditching your own nicotine habit—to encourage your tween not to light up. I'd love to be able to say that your own smoking won't affect or influence your kids, but I can't. Tweens and teens pay far more attention to what we do than what we say.

The Spiritual Lives of Tweens

Tweens have questions galore about God, but they are usually not deep, probing questions about theology. We have learned that the tweenage years are best for building the *foundational* skills of spiritual life. If they have no knowledge of the Bible at all, tweens need to learn who God is, why Jesus died, and how salvation is offered. We teach lessons and relate stories about the men and women of the Bible. We stress the importance of daily prayer and Bible reading because these devotional habits can last a lifetime.

Tweens from Christian homes need to learn the principles involved in choosing friends, building relationships with parents and other adults, making decisions, and maintaining a walk with Christ. It is also important for young people from Christian homes to have an opportunity to share their faith. Too many Christian young people are sheltered in private schools and so involved in church programs that they never have the opportunity to stand for Christ in the world. I once taught in a Christian school where in several of my classes students did not even know an unsaved person.

How do you get tweens excited about sharing Christ? We've found the best way is to encourage kids to concentrate on one or two unsaved friends. They can invite their friends to Sunday school or other church functions, make them feel welcome, and pray for them consistently. This type of friendship evangelism is very effective with tweens.

Give your tweens the chance to be a witness and a testimony for the Lord. Salt does no good if it is left in the saltshaker. Tweens need to practice standing in their faith, so let your children sign up for scouting, 4-H, Little League, or community gymnastics classes. They won't be surrounded by Christians in those environments, and they can learn to share their faith in those relatively protected situations. Let them learn to stand now, while a loving home is standing by to support them.

During this time tweens learn to reason and to accept, to question and to believe, to love and to lead. These are the years in which your kids will learn about God and put his promises to the test. They will learn to pray and wait for God's answers. During these years some kids will publicly identify themselves with Christ for the first time and receive either praise or scorn for their beliefs. It is not a good time to forsake church attendance or religious education. If you want your tween to grow into spiritual maturity, do not neglect spiritual teaching during the tweenage years.

Support Your Tween ...
Even When He's Embarrassed to Be Seen With You

Even if your tween would rather die than have you speak to him in public, do make every effort to attend his ball games, piano recitals, and science fairs. Your presence is worth more than any number of words you might utter, and taking time from your job to attend these functions tells your child that he is more important than your work. So, while it's not possible for both parents to be at every activity, do make an effort to attend your child's functions whenever possible.

Just (wink!) don't speak to him unless he speaks to you first.

Telephone

I'd just about had it with my thirteen-year-old daughter and her telephone habits. The minute Tiffany came through the door, the telephone seemed to latch onto her ear. She talked while she watched TV, she talked through dinner, and she talked on the phone while she was supposedly doing her homework. She'd talk until midnight if we'd let her!

My way of dealing with the situation was just to fuss, until I talked to a friend. She laughed and said she didn't have any hard and fast answers, but she did have an idea. To relieve the burden on the rest of the family, I should take a positive approach instead of a negative one. In addition, she urged me to consider the fact that as long as Tiffany was home talking on the phone, she wasn't out running around, she wasn't taking drugs, and she wasn't getting into really serious trouble. I realized I had allowed a minor thing to become a major hassle.

So, that night I went home and told Tiffany we were going to do something special. Because she loved the telephone so much, we were going to call the phone company and get a special telephone number just for her. Calls to that special number would be identified with a special ring, and no one would even pick up when we knew the call was for Tiffany. She could talk to her heart's content on this new telephone number.

In return for this privilege, Tiffany would have to meet a few responsibilities. Before she could begin her telephoning each afternoon, she'd have to finish her homework. Talking would also be forbidden at the dinner table and after 10:30 P.M. on school nights. With privileges comes responsibility, so if Tiffany wanted her own phone number (a very cool thing), she'd have to hold up her end of the bargain.

Tiffany received my suggestion with excitement, and so far everything seems to be going well. If this keeps up, I might even get her a new phone for her birthday. Something snazzy, maybe with glitter....

Three Pieces of Invaluable Advice

Dear Daughter:

I'm very glad that your teacher wants me to give you three pieces of advice. Here goes:

- *Always listen to your dad and me. You may not always like what we'll tell you, but God promises to bless you if you obey us—even if we're wrong. We would never intentionally do anything to hurt you; we want only what's best for you.*
- *Watch how boys treat their mothers. That's how they'll treat their wives. Your dad loved his mother a lot, and that's how I knew he'd be a great husband.*
- *Always wear pretty underwear—no one else will know, but you'll feel beautiful down to your skin.*

I love you very much,
Mom

The Totem Pole

Whether your community offers junior high schools or middle schools, your tween will face huge adjustments as he goes from being the "top man on the totem pole" in elementary school to the bottom of the middle school hierarchy. You can help your child with this adjustment in several ways.

First, go with your tween to school registration and quietly walk through the halls to locate his locker and classrooms. Make sure he knows his locker combination. Get a map of the school and study it together. Get your daughter a bra (whether or not she needs one) so she'll fit in with the other girls who change clothes for physical education. Offer a razor if all the other girls are shaving their legs.

Make sure your child leaves his childhood lunchbox at home. Watch the other kids and see how they're carrying their books and lunches to school—in a duffel bag, backpack, or just in a loose pile. To the best of your ability, make sure your tween can blend in comfortably.

Training

When Jessica was about fourteen, a thirteen-year-old boy began to call her. He was one of the cutest boys in our church youth group, and she was flattered by the attention. When I asked her if she liked him, she said, "He's really cute, Mom, and he's fun to be around, but I just don't think I have time to train him."

I asked her what she meant, and she explained that he had just started calling girls and didn't really know how to carry a conversation. He didn't understand the intricacies of the flirting game, either. Teaching him these things would take energy she wasn't sure she wanted to expend.

Three years later, after he had been adequately "trained," he tried again. This time he won her heart.

The Unspoken Pain of Abortion

Because so many teenagers become pregnant each year, I didn't feel this book would be complete without addressing the issue of abortion. So many parents, even Christian parents who would otherwise be against the forceful termination of a pregnancy, opt for convenience when their daughter becomes pregnant. The reasons most often given by teens for choosing abortion are being concerned about how a baby would change their lives, feeling that they are not mature enough to have a child, and having financial problems.[69]

Please, moms and dads, I beg you—talk to your sons and daughters about this issue. None of the above reasons are compelling enough to put your child and biological grandchild through the pain of abortion. As an adoptive parent myself, I know how precious that little life is, and I know there are millions of couples waiting now for the opportunity to adopt a child.

Abortion can be forgiven, of course, but the aftereffects can still be painful. The following letter is from my friend, Francine Rivers, author of *The Atonement Child*:

I am an expert on abortion. Believe me, I wish I weren't, but I had one over thirty years ago. That sin was one of the main reasons I didn't become a born-again Christian for so long. Even though I was reared in a Christian family, I thought I'd committed the unforgivable sin and there was no hope. It sure sounded that way when I encountered various Christians. It took me several years after being born again to deal with what I had done. I was going through a post-abortion class while writing *The Atonement Child*. That was the roughest year of writing I've ever had, but it was part of the healing process. I believe our society is permeated by the influences of abortion. For every child killed, there's a woman out there guilt-ridden, disillusioned, angry, anguished. And that's not counting the men who marry post-abortive women, or men who were part of the decision to abort a child, the children of these women, etc.

Abortion has a rippling effect. It's important that people realize it.

Francine Rivers

Values

If we are to counter the wave of media hype threatening to pull our children away from us, we must teach Christian values to our children. In a *St. Louis Post-Dispatch* article, children's author Mary Manz Simon says, "We have seen as a nation that core values are really important. It is an issue that transcends any kind of religious denominational affiliation."[70]

Where should a parent begin? Simon suggests the Ten Commandments. Life provides plenty of opportunities, she says, to teach bedrock values such as honesty, integrity, loyalty, kindness, and compassion, but too often we expect our children to absorb those values through environmental osmosis. "We have gotten lazy as parents," Simon says.[71]

A simple way to teach values is through the classic stories that illustrate them. William Bennett's *The Book of Virtues* ought to be required reading in every home long before the tweenage years arrive. It is filled with classic tales that can be read as bed-time stories, and each tale illustrates one of ten core values: self-discipline, compassion, responsibility, friendship, work, courage, perseverance, honesty, loyalty, and faith. The book and its stories would also make great material for family devotions.

Vocabulary

Every tween generation has its own vocabulary. A few years ago you couldn't converse with a middle schooler without hearing two hundred *likes* thrown into the dialogue: "It was like, this girl at school, is like, goofy-looking, and there was this guy, who's like, cool, and they're like, going out, or something...."

More recently, the catch phrase was "how (insert adjective

here) is that?" (Even my husband and I have picked it up. How pervasive is that?)

One mom told me that her middle school daughter went through a phase where she used only five phrases at home: "That's stupid," "What?," "I don't care," "Gross," and "What's for dinner?"

Don't worry, moms and dads. From what I understand, your kids will be back to speaking conversational English by the time they leave for college....

A Voice from the Past

Children today are tyrants. They contradict their parents, gobble their food, and tyrannize their teachers.

Socrates, 470-399 B.C.[72]

When Good Kids Go Bad

Every child spells trouble sometimes. But some children—especially in the adolescent years—can turn trouble into a pain-filled way of life for their families. Violence, profanity, crimes, substance abuse, sexual activity, refusing to abide by house rules—such irresponsible acts are in a different league from the usual parental challenges.

"These home-shaking disappointments make you understand why the word *rebellion* happens to contain the words *rebel* and *lion*," writes R.A. "Buddy" Scott in his book *Relief for Hurting Parents*. "Living with an out-of-control teenager can be like living with a lion on a rampage!"[73]

A few years ago, I had an opportunity to interview Buddy Scott about his practical and proven ideas for dealing with troubled teens. Scott has a special heart for parents who feel defeated by the bad choices made by a child they love. He has seen good Christian homes turned into war zones, leaving parents feeling confused, embarrassed, intimidated, and rejected. "Hurting parents," says Scott, "God knows how you feel. He lost his kids … and no one can say he didn't raise them right."[74]

I've shaped our interview into a "Q&A" format, and I hope Scott's insights will be helpful if you must deal with serious problems in the tween and teenage years.

Q: What are the signs that should indicate to parents that their child is headed toward serious trouble?

A: There are small indicators and huge indicators. An illustration will help me explain. If you look at a mountain range you can usually see foothills in the foreground and huge, jagged mountains in the background. The "foothills" are the small indicators—a child's withdrawal from the family, criticism of the traditional values of the family, and friendship with kids of lesser moral character. Also included among these foothills would be friends who call and won't give a full name, the rejection of the youth group at church, and fudging on curfew. In the foothills, a child is beginning to edge into wrong things, but he does it slowly and keeps his activities hidden.

In the jagged "mountains," though, teenagers don't come home at night, a girl skips school without her parents' knowledge, a boy comes home drunk, a best friend is arrested for dealing drugs. Or, a parent finds an incriminating note about sexual involvement or drug use.

Q: What are parents' typical reactions when trouble arises?

A: It depends on how kids rebel. Some kids are passively and secretly rebellious. They don't really want to hurt their parents. Other kids, however, are strong-willed, self-centered, and defiant. They don't care if they hurt their parents. They seem to care only about using their parents for as long as they can.

Parents' typical reaction to tyrannical teens is shock and trauma. They have tried to love their child unconditionally through crisis after crisis, so they ask, "This is our reward for trying faithfully?" Theirs is a different kind of hurt—it's worse than being fired after you've done your absolute best.

The misbehaviors of our children do not necessarily indicate that we are failures as parents. As parents we deserve respect. If we are seeking to heal our children and save them from damaging themselves morally, spiritually, emotionally, socially, and physically, we are *decent parents.*

Q: When a teen is in trouble, how should a parent react?

A: The best reaction is to see the situation as an opportunity to be a Christian witness to the child. So many times parents pick up Satan's tools to try to do God's work. They lose their tempers, plow into their kids with slaps and hits, or use curse words against their children. That approach simply will not work.

Parents should not reject their children in such ways. If you *reject* them, you will *eject* them toward the wrong crowd, and the wrong crowd will be happy to reel them in. We need to reject our kids' wrong behavior but reassure them of our love and trust. Parents have to let their kids know things can get better. They need to maintain their Christian witness to them. This gives them what I call a "decent environment for improvement."

Q: Is there a time when caring Christian parents should wash their hands of a child and let him go his own way?

A: I don't think there is a point when parents should leave their children without a Christian parental witness and just give them over to the world. It's very much like the kids are in a life raft and parents are the lifeline. You can't just cut the rope and forsake them. They have to know their parents still love and care for them.

But there is a point when parents should say, "I've done my best and now it's up to you. It's time for you to fly out of the nest. You can either fly and soar or fly and fall. If you fly and soar, I'll applaud. If you fly and fall, I'll pick you up if you really want help. But you won't just call and say, 'Can I come home?' The way back home is through family counseling or a treatment center."

Requiring counseling before wayward young adults

return home can avoid even more serious problems. Kids who are self-destructive can return to their parents looking desperate and tearfully pleading to be taken back into the home. Unfortunately, this often turns out to be only a vacation from their wrongs because they are still secretly unwilling to pay the price for change. Their parents nurse them back to health and then the kids go off and self-destruct some more. The parents were used.

Q: Parenting a child in trouble can be exhausting. Where are parents to find the strength to go through troubled days?

A: From understanding people who help them in their best attempt to rescue and recover their child, and from an understanding God.

Too many parents wonder why God won't answer their prayers and "fix" their problem. They wonder why God allowed it to happen. They don't realize that an understanding God is with them, and he is loving their child, too. God is not making a miracle to make the problems go away because he has promised every person free moral agency. He would have to barge into the child's control center and take over to answer many parents' prayers.

We pray astray when we ask God to do what he won't do. He didn't even barge in when Adam and Eve sinned—he let them exercise their rights as free moral agents. Free moral agency is really important to God, and we don't often understand that.

If the church is positive and supportive of a hurting family, the church can be a tremendous encouragement. If the church understands that good parents can have trouble with their kids, the church can be on the healing team by ministering to them. A truly loving church says,

"Even if you've made some mistakes, our position is to love you and support you."

In addition to God and the church, there needs to be a parent support group. There are support groups for all kinds of things, and our groups are just as vital as any others. Rebellion is not a disease, but a child who is rebelling is attacking himself and doing things against his own health. Certainly it is totally appropriate for that family to reach for help. With serious problems, parents are watching their kids decay and self-destruct right in front of them. There is nothing harder than that. Support groups should teach parents how to respond to the kids' offenses and bad attitudes with wiser reactions. All the parents in the group should want the same thing—to save their children. So a support group should offer pain relief, support, companionship, and guidance. All that comes together to give more confidence in parenting.

Q: What community and private resources are available for help?

A: Treatment centers must be investigated thoroughly. Many non-Christian substance-abuse centers, for example, are against their patients using alcohol or drugs. But patients can be profane, smoke, listen to the worst kinds of music, and be antagonistic toward their parents. And they are taught that sex outside of marriage is okay as long as they are sensitive to the other person's needs. It's often the blind trying to lead the blind and getting paid enormous fees for doing so. Recently, a man called me and said, "We placed my daughter in a non-Christian treatment program. They took away from her every Christian value we had and we paid them to do it. Now she's run away from home, and we have no money and no daughter."

What should you look for in a treatment center? You want a place that's clean and organized. You want therapists who have their lives and their integrity based upon the Rock of Jesus Christ instead of sand. The therapist should be loving, approachable, and someone who can relate to your child on an emotional level. Look for the therapist's credentials and ask about his work experience. Finally, you want a program that has already established a good reputation for helping and healing adolescents.

Unless your child has evidenced suicidal gestures, dangerous behavioral problems, criminal behavioral problems, or severe drug or alcohol addiction, you should probably investigate reliable counseling instead of a treatment center. A study was done with 500 delinquent kids, half of whom received secular counseling. At age thirty, the 250 kids who had received no counseling had had fewer divorces and higher paying jobs. Some think the problem was that those who did receive help were made to feel they had problems. To keep this from happening, I've frequently referred to myself as a "life coach" instead of a "counselor."

Q: After a family has confronted their problems and gone through whatever measures are necessary, how can they be sure their son or daughter does not lapse again?

A: If you are really committed to saving your children, you must see that two changes occur: a change of mind-set and a change of crowd. Unless both occur, there will not be a permanent change. The enemy to the change of mind-set is the wrong crowd. I have never—not a single time—seen a kid change and stay changed unless his parents required a complete break with the wrong crowd. In fact, the Bible establishes that "evil company corrupts good habits" (1 Corinthians 15:33, NKJV).

Christian friends are essential. If your child goes through counseling or treatment and comes out wanting to try his best to succeed, and Christian kids are faithful to him, he will change his crowd. This change can give more assurance that his conversion from degeneration to regeneration will be permanent.

Moms and dads, there are lots of good parenting books available, but Buddy Scott's *Relief for Hurting Parents* is unique (Allon Publishing, ISBN 0-963-76450-0). I highly recommend this book for anyone who encounters bumps in the road as they parent tweens and teens. Order from your local bookstore or from Amazon.com.

Teaching Tweens to Make Wise Choices

I suppose every mother faces this situation sooner or later ... seems to me that I put my mother through the exact same thing. But on a Saturday night when my husband was out of town, I was pacing in the living room and watching the clock. Eleven o'clock, and I had no idea where my fourteen-year-old daughter was.

I knew she'd gone to a football game with some kids from school. But the game should have been over ages ago ... so where was my kid?

I called a friend, but no one answered. I called the athletic director at the school and confirmed my fears—the game had ended at nine-thirty. I finally called another woman I didn't know, but whose daughter was a good friend of my daughter's. "Oh, after the game they went to Kaycee's house," the woman told me. "They were giving one of their teachers a surprise birthday party."

I jotted down the address for Kaycee's house, then jumped into my car and drove, taking deep breaths in order to keep my blood from boiling. When I pulled into the driveway of Kaycee's house (whoever Kaycee was), I asked some kids loitering outside if they'd seen my daughter. A moment later, out she came, waving goodbye to her friends as casually as if we'd arranged this little pickup.

The smile faded when she got into the car. I immediately launched into Mother Sermon #405, the one that begins, "If you're going somewhere else, you must call and ask permission. I worry about you, I love you, and I want to know where you are at all times...."

She tearfully explained that it wasn't a big deal, it was a nice party, with lots of adults and nothing bad going on. And it was only eleven o'clock, so why was I so upset?

"You've got to think of people other than yourself," I told her. "Sometimes that just means taking a moment to call. You've got to know that I was home worrying about you. Learn to make wise decisions, honey, and you'll make life easier for both of us."

As tweens begin to function independently of mom and dad, they are faced with choices about everything from accepting a ride home with an older student to using drugs. Sometimes they choose right and deserve praise; sometimes they choose wrong and deserve a rebuke. But you can teach your children to make wise choices in everything if you teach them the following guidelines. There are five, one for each finger, and you can encourage your child to memorize them as he counts them down.

1. If I do this, will I be disobeying someone God has placed over me?

2. Will doing this harm my body?
3. Will this decision hurt someone else?
4. Will I be glad I did this tomorrow?
5. Could I do this if Jesus were standing beside me right now?

The World

In John 17:15-19, Jesus prayed:

> I'm not asking you to take them out of the world, but to keep them safe from the evil one. They are not part of this world any more than I am. Make them pure and holy by teaching them your words of truth. As you sent me into the world, I am sending them into the world. And I give myself entirely to you so they also might be entirely yours.

The Savior's prayer might well be the prayer of every Christian parent. We want to teach our children to be independent and spiritually mature, and in the light of those goals we must see that we cannot make every decision for them, nor can we dictate rules for their lives without ever teaching them the reasons behind the rules.

I love my children. But I know that one day soon I must send them out into the world, so I want them to be prepared for and inoculated against evil.

Have you ever thought about how an inoculation works? Take smallpox, for instance: the patient is injected with a small amount of the cowpox virus, which causes the body to produce antibodies that resist the cowpox *and* smallpox. Exposure to a relatively harmless virus gives protection against a deadly germ.

You may not agree with what I'm about to suggest, and I'd be the first to say that you will have to be sensitive to the Lord's leading in your own life, but let me demonstrate how this vaccination principle has worked in our family.

When the movie *Pocahontas* came out, several mothers in our church told me they wouldn't take their children to see it because the movie contained examples of pantheism, the worship of nature. I respected their convictions. Yet I took my children, and on the way home from the movie I explained that yes, the Native American tribes did worship nature. They did believe in the spirits of the trees and the wind, but Pocahontas (who was probably but a tween herself when she met John Smith) married the Englishman John Rolfe, became a Christian, and was baptized in England. She grew up believing in the spirits of nature, but then she met the true God. The *real* Pocahontas realized she had been worshiping the creation rather than the Creator.

Years later, the movie *Titanic* was a particular hit with tween girls. Leonardo DeCaprio became an overnight sensation among the ten-to-fourteen set, and nearly every girl in our middle school department saw the PG-13 movie at least twice. While I had a few friends who flatly refused to allow their children to see it, I took my fourteen-year-old daughter and we saw it together. Later we talked about how much was historical and how much fiction, and we also talked about the wisdom of the heroine's decision to have sex with the hero. "It would have been so much better for her to find the preacher on the ship and marry Jack," I pointed out. "And then she wouldn't have had to worry about confronting her cruel fiancé. The marriage would have been a done deal ... but that probably wouldn't have made as exciting a movie. They invent things, you see, to make movies more interesting, but what we see on the screen doesn't always reflect real life."

Parents have to use wisdom and discernment. My fourteen-year-old daughter could handle the lessons of *Titanic*, but I didn't think it was a good idea for my thirteen-year-old son to see that film, and for entirely different reasons. I didn't want him to be confronted with the nude model/artist scene. Each child is different, and you have to make decisions accordingly.

Our kids have to live in the world, so we'd better equip them to think things through. Personally, I'd rather explain the facts of life and the world to my tween than forfeit my position to her peers, television, movies, and popular magazines. In each situation and with each child you should seek the Holy Spirit's leading in your life.

Worrywarts

Probably the most consistent emotional state in the tween years is worry. Holly, a sixth-grader, says she worries about "not getting a date." She won't be allowed to date until she's sixteen, but she's worrying now.

Mike, an eighth-grader, says he worries about "getting rejected by friends and being laughed at."

Elizabeth says, "I worry about my grades. I get upset when I see a C or a D. I think, 'I could have studied more,' or, 'What a foolish, careless mistake.'"

One boy told researcher Louise Bates Ames, "Most of the time I worry that people won't like me. I worry that I'm going to worry. I worry that I should stop worrying."[75]

Tweens worry about friends, money, family, and growing up. They worry about their report cards, acne, and braces. They worry about being fat, being clumsy, and being left out. They worry that they will never have a boyfriend or girlfriend, that their freckles are too prevalent, and that their clothes are out of style. They worry that their parents will get a divorce. They worry about going to hell, driving a car, and being embarrassed.

Boys worry about not making the team. Being part of a team is a definite status symbol—it means you have worth, that you are skilled, desirable, and a cut above the ordinary. But, if the boy makes the team, he worries about making a mistake, costing the team the game, or looking funny as he plays the sport. He feels clumsy, disjointed, and awkward. He worries that if he gets hurt he will cry—and the embarrassment of crying is worse than the pain of injury. He worries that he will be called "sissy" by the coach or the other players. He worries that his father won't be proud of him. He worries that his father will—or won't—come to the game … and that if his father does show up he'll play poorly.

Girls worry about not looking right. They worry about their clothes and their friends. A girl might be jealous when a new girl comes to school—what if the newcomer decides to take away her best friend? What happens if her boyfriend decides to like the new girl? If Mom buys Daughter a new outfit and Daughter doesn't know of someone—an *acceptable* someone—who has one just like it, she is hesitant to wear it.

Girls gaze wistfully at the more-developed older girls and wish their breasts would hurry and grow. Girls worry about the spurt of growth which causes them to grow taller than the boys and stretches their feet longer than they are supposed to be. Girls worry about wearing bowling shoes and skates that boldly display their shoe size; they worry about starting their periods in school. They worry about wearing a bra or not wearing one. They worry because they do not measure up to the pencil-slim models in fashion magazines and the skinny actresses featured in nearly every television sitcom.

At school, tweens worry about forgetting their locker combination and being late to class. Often they will experience headaches or upset stomachs before school, tryouts, and tests. If your child complains of an upset stomach on several occasions and has no fever, it may be time for a heart-to-heart talk about what could be worrying him.

If your tween has lost last year's circle of friends, he may be anxious about making new friends. If your daughter has transferred from a small elementary school to a large middle school, she may be petrified at the thought of losing her way between classes. If your son had difficulty with academics in the lower grades, he may be struggling with a feeling of hopelessness as he faces subjects like algebra and chemistry.

Kids worry about things at home, too. I've heard the following from tweens in our group:

- "When my parents fight, I worry that they'll be getting a divorce and I'll have to choose between them."
- "My older sister keeps threatening to kill herself. I feel like I should do something, but I don't know what to do."
- "My kid brother gets all the attention. I really don't care anymore, but I worry that my parents don't love me as much as they love him."
- "My parents are always saying, 'We can't afford that.' Sometimes I worry that we won't be able to pay the bills or that we'll have to move out of our house."
- "My dad is always sick, or at least he says he is. I'm worried that he's going to have a heart attack and die."
- "My mother drinks constantly. I think she's an alcoholic, and I worry that she'll go out in a car and kill somebody someday … maybe even me."
- "I think my brother is using drugs. His friends don't seem all that great, but he likes them better than he likes us. I'm afraid he's going to end up in jail."

Home—the place that should bring welcome relief from the cares of a harsh and demanding world—is often the greatest source of pressure and worry for a tween.

How's your home? No family exists in a perfect environment, but when difficulties come, do you resort to worry or prayerful faith? When you are beset by trials, do you fret or rest in confidence of the Lord's faithfulness? Your children are watching, and even in this worrisome tween age they will look to you as an example.

How do you help your child overcome worry? First, try to understand what your tween is feeling when he worries. Assure him that he is not alone—you worried about things when you were younger, too. The other kids at school, even the coolest kids, sometimes feel insecure.

One key to overcoming worry is preparation. If your son worries about taking tests, make sure he studies for those tests so he can be as prepared as possible. Like the tween who made copies of her schedule and taped them to all her notebooks, help your tween to be prepared for life in middle school.

Another key to overcoming worry is acceptance. The things we can't change must be accepted. If your daughter worries that her red hair is all wrong, help her accept her hair color as a gift from God. Point out other striking redheads, and let her see that her uniqueness may become her greatest asset.

Sit down with your tween one day and have her make a list of all her worries. Tell her to hold nothing back, but to write down everything—and promise not to read the list. When your tween is finished, have her mark the things she can change or work on, then lead her in a prayer to turn the other things over to God.

Finally, have your worrier memorize the following verses. Type them up on a note card and place them on the refrigerator and the bathroom mirror. You might even slip small copies into your tween's lunch bag.

- "So I tell you, don't worry about everyday life—whether you have enough food, drink, and clothes. Doesn't life consist of more than food and clothing?" (Matthew 6:25)
- "Don't worry about anything; instead, pray about everything. Tell God what you need, and thank him for all he has done" (Philippians 4:6).
- "Give all your worries and cares to God, for he cares about what happens to you" (1 Peter 5:7).

Xeroderma, Xerophyte, Xenophobe

Well, I really had to scratch my head when I reached this particular letter of the alphabet. After considering all of the above words (meaning dry skin, a desert plant, and someone who's fearful of foreigners, respectively), I decided to go with

Xavier Cugat

What does Xavier Cugat have to do with life as a middle school mom? Not much, but I'll admit his was the first name that popped into my brain when I considered the letter "x." Xavier Cugat, for those of you who need reminding, was the Spanish bandleader and actor who introduced the Rumba to the United States. He died in October 1990, at the generous age of ninety. (Apparently the Rumba is good for the circulatory system.)

What I want you to remember about Xavier is this—he went through the tweenage years. He put his mother through the same situations you and I are living through now. And if Xavier can survive and live to make a rhythmic mark on the world, your kid will make it, too. So will mine.

With God's help, we'll all make it through.

One X-tra Bit of Advice

Don't believe everything you read. Take every piece of advice—including mine—under prayerful consideration, but follow your own instincts when dealing with your child. After all, you and your spouse know your kid better than anyone else does.

If you're looking for a foolproof way to parent tweens, you'll be looking a *long* time. A 1995 report from the Carnegie Council on Adolescent Development focusing on ten- to fourteen-year-olds reported: "A social consensus holds that knowledge about infant and child development is critical to a child's future. No such consensus yet exists in defining the knowledge parents should have about the adolescent years or about their roles during that critical period."[76]

Imagine! The experts who study such things are admitting that no one knows the best way to parent tweens. I believe the best you can do is love your kids, be sure the boundaries are clearly defined, and instill the principles of God's Word. Pray when times get tough, and try to insure that when your kids aren't talking to you, they *are* talking to other adults you trust.

Finally, as one of my fellow mothers has already said, rest in the realization that God loves your little sparrow even more than you do.

Youth Workers

The youth workers in your church will help encourage the spiritual life of your tween during these crucial years. Take the time to meet and talk with your child's youth pastor or Sunday school teacher. Volunteer whenever possible, but give your child plenty of space if he or she seems reluctant to have you participate.

A good youth worker supports parents, recognizes that all families are different, and keeps the lines of communication open between parents, tweens, and the church. Your church staff, however, cannot be held responsible for every problem in your child's life. They can help, and God can work miracles, but you cannot blame your church if your child learns about right and wrong—and chooses to do wrong.

Finally, do not take your youth minister's job lightly. He or she is more than a babysitter and activities director. Every time my husband goes on an activity with tweens and teens, I realize that he is responsible for their lives. Accidents do happen, and often the youth leader is powerless to prevent them. Kids disobey, and sometimes they get hurt.

Pray for those teachers, youth leaders, and volunteers who give of their lives to work with your children. They are sacrificing their time because they love your children, too.

Zits

The most successful new comic to hit daily newspapers is "Zits," created by Jim Borgman and Jerry Scott. The cartoon, which features life with a fifteen-year-old boy named Jeremy, built a syndication list of over 425 newspapers in just six months—an unheard-of feat. Carl Crothers, managing editor of the *Winston-Salem Journal*, says the strip "pushes a button with so many people who have teenagers.... Even if you're not the parent of a teenager, you were a teenager once. Everyone can relate to being embarrassed by parents and other coming-of-age issues. The strip is absolutely realistic."[77]

How do the comic strip's creators guarantee such realism? First, Jim Borgman runs the strips by his fifteen-year-old son, Dylan. The comic's creators also study teenagers' hair, clothing, speech, and idiosyncrasies. The daughter of a friend of Jim's once photographed her friends, then shared the photos with Borgman, carefully explaining the subtle, unspoken clues that proclaimed each teen's social group. To study teens' hand-writing and doodles, Borgman asked his son to sift through school garbage cans for old student notebooks. Borgman and Scott have also parked across the street from their local high schools and sketched teens as they swarmed out of school at the closing bell.[78]

So, moms and dads, if you're ever feeling that no one else understands what you're going through in this parenting business, open your newspaper to the comic page and read "Zits."

It's *wonderful* to know you're not alone.

About the Author

When she's not helping her husband in youth ministry or chauffeuring her teenagers, Angela Elwell Hunt is a novelist and author of more than seventy titles for children and adults. For more information on her books, visit her web page:
www.AngelaElwellHunt.com

You may write her in care of this publisher, or e-mail her at Angie@AngelaElwellHunt.com.

Notes

1. B.B. Brown, M.J. Lohr, and E.L. McLenahan, "Early Adolescents' Perceptions of Peer Pressure," *Journal of Early Adolescence*, 6:139–54.
2. Barbara Kantrowitz and Pat Wingert, "The Truth About Tweens," *Newsweek*, October 18, 1999, 69.
3. Elaine Carey, "Tweens," *Toronto Star*, December 6, 1998.
4. Carey.
5. Charles Schulz, quoted in *The Third—and Possibly the Best—637 Best Things Anybody Ever Said* (New York: Atheneum, 1986), number 171.
6. Chris J. Boyatzis, Peggy Baloff, and Cheri Durieux, "Effects of Perceived Attractiveness and Academic Success on Early Adolescent Peer Popularity," *Journal of Genetic Psychology*, September 1, 1998, 337.
7. Boyatzis, Baloff, and Durieux, 337.
8. Jean Perron, "Boring Means Many Things for Tweens," *Wisconsin State Journal*, January 8, 1995.
9. Bill Cosby, quoted in *The Third—and Possibly the Best—637 Best Things Anybody Ever Said* (New York: Atheneum, 1986), number 170.
10. Linda Simpson, Sara Douglas, and Julie Schimmel, "Tween Consumers: Catalog Clothing Purchase Behavior," *Adolescence*, September 22, 1998.
11. James Dobson, "The Most Difficult Period of Adolescence," *Parents and Teenagers* (Wheaton, Ill.: Victor, 1984), 157.
12. Jennifer Emily, "Family Does Its Part to Protect Childhood," *Dallas Morning News*, October 24, 1999, 1S.
13. Josh McDowell, *Why Wait?* (San Bernardino, Calif.: Here's Life, 1987), 79.

14. Adapted from Buddy Scott's *Relief for Hurting Parents* (Nashville, Tenn.: Thomas Nelson, 1989), 28.
15. Adapted from "Hey Girls—Look What Alcohol Can Do for You" (Silver Spring, Md.: National Federation of Parents for a Drug-Free Youth).
16. Charlene C. Giannetti and Margaret Sagarese, *The Roller-Coaster Years* (New York: Broadway, 1997), 82.
17. Edward C. Martin, "The Early Adolescent in School," in *12 to 16: Early Adolescence* (New York: W.W. Norton, 1972), 190.
18. Giannetti and Sagarese, 158.
19. Maggie Gallagher, "Yielding to the Tweening Influence," *Washington Times*, October 19, 1999.
20. Gallagher.
21. Mary Pipher, quoted in Jennifer Hunter's "Goodbye Girlhood: Entering Puberty Early Brings Heavy Baggage," *MacLean's*, March 22, 1999, 47.
22. Jennifer Emily, "Today's 'Tweens' More Savvy about Adult Matters: Movies, TV Shows Playing Role, One Psychologist Says," *Dallas Morning News*, October 24, 1999, 1S.
23. Suzanne Fields, "Growing Up on Fast Forward," *Washington Times*, January 4, 1999, A17.
24. Personal interview with Dr. Clyde Narramore, April 28, 1986, Lynchburg, Virginia.
25. Fields, A17.
26. Carey.
27. Gallagher.
28. Anne Bratskeir, "Girls Just Want to Grow Up," *Newsday*, September 1, 1999, B06.
29. Shawna Steinberg, "Have Allowance, Will Transform Economy," *Canadian Business*, March 13, 1998, 58.
30. A. Cuneo, "Targeting Tweens: Madison Avenue's Call of the Child," *U.S. News & World Report*, March 10, 1989, 84–85.
31. Steinberg, 58.
32. Kay S. Hymowitz, *Ready or Not: Why Treating Children as Small Adults Endangers Their Future—and Ours*, Free Press,

1999, quoted in "Family Times; Quotables," *Washington Times*, November 9, 1999, E2.

33. Ellen Edwards, *Washington Post* staff writer, "Plugged-In Generation: More Than Ever, Kids Are at Home With Media," *Washington Post*, November 18, 1999, A01.

34. Edwards. According to Edwards, while time spent on the computer lags far behind time spent on TV use, among tweens who use a computer for recreation, the average use was fifty-two minutes per day.

35. Edwards.

36. Steinberg, 58.

37. Edwards.

38. Richard Zoglin, reported by Jordan Bonfante and Martha Smilgis/Los Angeles and Janice C. Simpson/New York, "Cover Stories: Sitcom Politics," *Time*, September 21, 1992, 44.

39. Edwards.

40. Edwards.

41. Edwards.

42. Carey.

43. Carey.

44. Carey.

45. Bratskeir, B06.

46. Scott, 25–26.

47. Gallagher.

48. Giannetti and Sagarese, xvi.

49. Urie Bronfenbrenner, *The Ecology of Human Development* (Cambridge: Harvard University Press, 1979), 284.

50. John Janeway Conger, "A World They Never Knew," in *12 to 16: Early Adolescence* (New York: W.W. Norton, 1972), 22.

51. William Bennett, speech given at Liberty University, Lynchburg, Virginia, April 23, 1986.

52. Adapted from Connie Marshner's *Decent Exposure: How to Teach Your Children About Sex* (Brentwood, Tenn.: Wolgemuth & Hyatt, 1988), 177–78.

53. Arthur L. Stinchcombe, *Rebellion in a High School* (Chicago:

(Quadrangle Books, 1964), referred to by David Bakan in "Adolescence in America," in *12 to 16: Early Adolescence* (New York: W.W. Norton, 1972), 84.

54. Michael Thompson, quoted in Suzanne Field's "Growing Up on Fast Forward," *Washington Times,* January 4, 1999, A17.

55. S. Singh and J.E. Darroch, "Trends in Sexual Activity Among Adolescent American Women: 1982-1995," *Family Planning Perspectives,* 31, no. 5 (1999): 211-19.

56. Alan Guttmacher Institute, *Sex and America's Teenagers* (New York: Alan Guttmacher Institute, 1994), 19-20.

57. K.A. Moore, et al., *A Statistical Portrait of Adolescent Sex, Contraception, and Childbearing* (Washington, D.C.: National Campaign to Prevent Teen Pregnancy, 1998), 11.

58. Moore, et al.

59. Alan Guttmacher Institute, *Sex and America's Teenagers* (New York, 1994), 38.

60. P. Donovan, *Testing Positive: Sexually Transmitted Disease and the Public Health Response* (New York: Alan Guttmacher Institute, 1993), 24.

61. Alan Guttmacher Institute, "Teenage Pregnancy: Overall Trends and State-by-State Information" (New York: Alan Guttmacher Institute, 1999), table 1.

62. S.J. Ventura et al., "Births: Final Data for 1997," *National Vital Statistics Report,* 1997, vol. 47, no. 18, table 2.

63. Alan Guttmacher Institute, "Teenage Pregnancy: Overall Trends and State-by-State Information," table 1.

64. Personal interview with Connie Marshner, July 5, 1988.

65. Personal interview with Surgeon General C. Everett Koop, January 18, 1987.

66. Marshner interview.

67. Jane Lovatt, "Little Madam's Makeover," *Independent on Sunday,* February 21, 1999, 4.

68. Personal interview with Surgeon General Koop.

69. A. Torres and J.D. Forrest, "Why do Women Have Abortions?" *Family Planning Perspectives,* 20, no. 4 (1988): 169–76, table 1.

174

70. Robert Goodrich, "Parents Without Values Can't Teach Them to Teens, Writer Says," *St. Louis Post-Dispatch*, May 13, 1999.

71. Goodrich.

72. Socrates, quoted in *The Third—and Possibly the Best—637 Best Things Anybody Ever Said* (New York: Atheneum, 1986), number 164.

73. Scott, 10.

74. Personal interview with Buddy Scott, Feb. 6, 1990.

75. Louise Bates Ames, Frances Ilg, and Sidney Baker, "A Parent's Guide to the Tween Years," *Redbook*, June 1988, 150.

76. Giannetti and Sagarese, xiii.

77. David Astor, "Why 'Zits' Zoomed up the Sales Charts," *Editor & Publisher*, February 28, 1998, 28.

78. *Raising Teens*, Fall 1999, 40–41.